The

BALANCE
MYTH

RETHINKING WORK-LIFE SUCCESS

TERESA A. TAYLOR

GREENLEAF
BOOK GROUP PRESS

Published by Greenleaf Book Group Press
Austin, Texas
www.gbgpress.com

Distributed by Greenleaf Book Group, LLC

For ordering information or special discounts for bulk purchases, please
contact Greenleaf Book Group LLC at PO Box 91869, Austin, TX 78709,
512.891.6100.

Design and composition by Greenleaf Book Group, LLC
Cover design by Greenleaf Book Group, LLC
Cover credits: High heel copyright ©Lisa A, 2012. Used under license from
Shutterstock.com; tennis shoe ©Veer/Wong Sze Fei.

Publisher's Cataloging-In-Publication Data
(Prepared by The Donohue Group, Inc.)
Taylor, Teresa A.
  The balance myth : rethinking work-life success / Teresa A. Taylor. -- 1st ed.
    p. ; cm.
  Issued also as an ebook.
  ISBN: 978-1-60832-564-1 (hardcover)
  1. Work and family--Psychological aspects. 2. Women in the professions-
-Conduct of life. 3. Women in the professions--Family relationships--
Psychological aspects. 4. Married women--Employment--Psychological
aspects. 5. Success--Psychological aspects. I. Title.
HD4904.25 .T39 2013
306.3/61   2012954178

Part of the Tree Neutral® program, which offsets the number of trees
consumed in the production and printing of this book by taking
proactive steps, such as planting trees in direct proportion to the
number of trees used: www.treeneutral.com

Printed in the United States of America on acid-free paper

13 14 15 16 17 18   10 9 8 7 6 5 4 3 2 1

First Edition

To the special men in my life
Pete, Jack, and Joe
Thank you for your relentless encouragement and support

CONTENTS

ACKNOWLEDGMENTS

A chance encounter with a tremendous writer, Summer Poole, was a major catalyst to this book's journey to print. Thank you to Summer for providing guidance, insight, thoughtfulness, and most importantly for listening. I wish her the best as she continues her journey.

My sincere thanks to all the US West/Qwest men and women whom I have worked with—I have learned from each one of them and I am thankful that our paths crossed over the years. Many of these people continue to be lifetime friends. Specifically I would like to call out Dick Notebaert and Ed Mueller, the last two CEOs during my tenure at Qwest. Dick and Ed believed in me and pushed me beyond what I thought I was capable of. I am eternally grateful for their mentorship and insight. I also want to acknowledge the "whispering" that their wives, Peggy and Susan, provided to me when they witnessed me struggling.

Many friends contributed to this book by allowing me to include them in my stories, by listening, and by giving me constructive feedback. A specical acknowledgment to Robin Doerr, my lifetime best friend. Thank you to each and every one of you.

My mother was instrumental in shaping who I am today. I acknowledge her admirable strength and perseverance. The Thome family: Ann, Dick, Mark, Brian, and Karen, became a part of my family at an early age and I want to call them out for all of their involvement and guidance. In particular, Brian and Darcy have allowed me, Pete, and our sons the privilege of returning the love to them and their three children.

Pete's older brothers—Jim, Bob, and Tom—have always been truly interested in my career and I thank them for their encouragement. They participated in the ups and downs and were always enthusiastic as my career

ACKNOWLEDGMENTS

took off. A special thanks to Terry, Kelly, and Megan for helping my boys appreciate the female perspective.

Most important, I would like to thank my family for their patience, encouragement, and wisdom during my writing process. I started out with a simple goal of writing a book and little did I know that it would be such an experience for all of us. I will forever be grateful to my husband Pete and my two sons, Jack and Joe, for riding this roller coaster with me. They contributed, guided, and laughed with me along the way.

PROLOGUE

"I'm just a C at everything."

Her words didn't surprise me. I had seen her earlier, peeking out from behind the attendees who had crowded around me at the end of my speech. I recognized the hungry look on her face. As I talked with the dispersing crowd, I could feel her fixed gaze. Finally, as I was walking toward the exit doors, she sprinted to catch up and introduced herself.

"I have about five minutes if you want to walk with me on the way to my car," I offered. "What's on your mind?"

She took a deep breath. "I listened to your speech. I know about your career, but I can't figure it out. You have a family and a career, but you didn't compromise either. I don't get it. How did you do it?"

I glanced at my watch. I needed more than five minutes to help her, but five minutes was all I really had. I stopped walking and gave her my full attention.

"I'm just so overwhelmed," she began, coming to a halt with a lurch. "I'm struggling to balance the demands I have at work with the time I need to spend at home with my husband and daughter." Her sigh sounded like it would cut her open. "My daughter's closer to her nanny than she is to me."

Though I had not struggled with feelings of being cut off from my husband and sons, I had no difficulty putting myself in her shoes. And I had one particularly painful memory of my own: A teacher had assumed I was my son's nanny rather than his mother because she had never seen me before. It had felt like a punch to the gut.

"I'm just a C at everything," she repeated. "I'm a C as a wife. I'm a C as a mother." She groaned. "I absolutely get a C at my job. I just can't do it all!"

"I understand that overwhelmed feeling," I said. "I

remember all the guilt and agony I put myself through over the years."

"You do?" Her eyes looked me over with disbelief, as if I couldn't have gone through the same struggles she faced, as if inside my purse I was hiding an old magic checklist that had put me securely on the path of least resistance. Her eyes pleaded with me, wanting me to say, "Oops, sorry! I can't believe I forgot to share this with you! Here it is."

What she needed was for me to have more than five minutes to explain a few things to her. She wanted me to invest in her success. What she couldn't know was how much I wanted to as well.

I frowned and glanced again at my watch. Now I had four minutes left. I knew from experience that it was going to take me much longer than that just to get her to believe that there had been no magic involved. I held back an exasperated sigh; I didn't have time for subtlety, and I had to give her something of value to take away. "First, you have to stop being so hard on yourself. Tell yourself that you're not a C; you're an A."

She just blinked.

"I'm serious. Stop thinking of your life as something that must be graded and measured. That just makes it harder than it needs to be. Go ahead and tell yourself that you're an A already."

Her brow furrowed. "But I'm not an A," she said, as if I hadn't heard her earlier admission. "I'm not doing that well. I'm average at best. I work hard, but I feel like I'm always fighting spot fires—"

"Doesn't matter. Give yourself an A anyway."

She shook her head. "But—"

I didn't have time for buts. "I mean it! As women, we are much too hard on ourselves. It's ridiculous. Why do you think you deserve a C?"

Her answer was ready. "I can't seem to find the right balance between work and home."

And there it was: that insidious word, *balance*. If we'd had more time, I'm sure I would have heard the word *trade-off* come out of her mouth as well. I felt my watch ticking on my wrist. I needed to keep my answers simple. "All right. Here's number two. *Balance* is a horrible word. That and *trade-off* are two words that fester and set women up for failure every time. Try not to think of your life as a zero-sum game or as an equation that has to be balanced."

She looked at me as if I'd gone crazy. "But then how do I—"

"Let me ask you a question," I interrupted. "What is it, exactly, that makes you feel like you're a C? I mean what, specifically, is giving you the most heartburn?"

She considered this. "I think, overall, my main problem is that I'm not a very good multitasker."

Oh yeah. *Multitasking!* One more word to hate. I smiled at my reaction.

"I need to be better at it," she continued, quickly outlining how she envisioned implementing that skill in her work life. "I need to be more effective with my time."

"Yes. Time management is huge. But let's be even more specific," I tried. I turned and began to walk toward my car. She jogged to keep up. I needed to shift her focus away from work. Like many career women I had talked to over the years, she was determined to focus on work first, but most of these women had issues that originated at home. I repeated again: "Can you give me an example of something—some specific situation—that makes you feel like you're not a good multitasker? Maybe you're having trouble getting your daughter off to school in the morning, and that's making you late for work. Maybe something at home like that. Can you identify your main stumbling block?"

We had reached my car. I turned to her and waited. She still didn't—couldn't—answer. The nerve I had hit was obviously a raw one.

I pulled my keys out of my purse, trying to delay for as long as possible.

Finally she let out her breath as her cheeks flushed. "My husband isn't great at helping me at home. I feel like I have to manage everything without his help or input."

"That's really hard for you to deal with, right?"

She nodded.

"Then you've made my last point for me. The fact is that if you have issues in your life at home, it's going to distract you in every other part of your life, no matter how hard you try elsewhere."

Her eyes teared up. *Bingo*.

"Listen." I tried to make my voice sound light. I wanted to leave her with something positive. "You're not alone in this. We're all dealing with some sort of issue that makes it hard for us to get everything done that we need to. During my career, if my kids were sick, I was thinking about my kids. I may have been present at work, but I was only half listening while I waited for the doctor to call. And if it was a disagreement with my husband? Well, then, it went to the office with me, too. When I was tense from whatever was going on at home, I felt tenser at work also. These things just stay on your mind."

She cleared her throat. "So what did you do?"

Offer a Band-Aid. "I was honest with myself and faced my problems at home first, without masking them with the excuse of my job."

She visibly swallowed.

I took another breath. "If the main issue is with your

husband, then start there, with your marriage. Make *that* the priority. Get *that* to where you want it to be, *wherever that place is*, and everything else in your family and your professional life will eventually fall into place."

Her eyes narrowed as she considered what I said. "I'm not saying that it's easy or that it doesn't take a lot of work!" I continued. "But after your work day is over, *your* child and *your* husband are waiting for you. You really can't have success in one area of your life without having success in the other." I unlocked my car door. "I'm sorry I don't have more time."

Her face visibly softened. "Oh, no. I understand. I really appreciate your time."

I reached out and touched her forearm, still not satisfied with our conversation. "Going forward, remember to keep it simple. Choose one thing and focus on just that."

"I'll try. Thanks for your time, really. I don't know what I expected. It was kind of a loaded question to throw at you, but . . . I was sitting in the audience and I couldn't get over how confident you sounded when you talked about your family, how you seemed to have no need to apologize. Thanks for letting me bother you."

"It was no bother," I said as I opened the car door. "Start simple." I felt my smile widen. "I promise. It can be done."

Her face brightened. "I've wondered sometimes. Again, I really appreciate your time." She turned and started to walk back to the conference hall.

As I drove out of the garage, I was agitated and frustrated. It wasn't with how late I was going to be for my next appointment, but rather that the five minutes and a jog to my car was only enough time to tell that young woman the basic idea of what I wanted to tell her, not to qualify and quantify it. I wanted to show her where the bodies were buried, what mistakes to avoid, and what pitfalls to sidestep.

I gripped the wheel a little harder. I knew the woman had been seeing the same mirage that others had seen, the mirage that I had somehow arrived at my current level of success without any difficulty. That I was somehow different than they were. But I was no different than any of them. Early in my career, I had to seek out mentors as well. I had to learn difficult lessons both on and off the job, and a lot of those lessons were hard earned.

I also wanted her to believe—I still want her to believe—that she doesn't have to choose between being a great wife and mother and being a career woman. She can have both. The answers she's searching for are not in some magic checklist, but rather within herself, if she will just take the time to look for them.

But she also has to have the confidence to reach for them and believe they'll be there.

The shame the young woman felt was the opposite of that confidence. It would drive her to second-guess herself and the decisions she would have to make in the hope of keeping both of her worlds what she had called "balanced."

Which is why I subscribe to this: You are the same person all the way through. You can't be one person in one environment and then switch to a completely different person as your circumstances or situations change. If you try to separate yourself from yourself in that way, you're always going to struggle, because integrity, morality, and desires have little to do with the situation you're dealing with and everything to do with your personal authenticity.

True success is living an accomplished life and making sure that life is fully lived. To think in terms of "balance" would require us to make a trade-off between one life and another. Instead, if your work life is challenging, take energy from your home and put it into work. If your home life is difficult, give yourself a break at work so you can focus on home. I couldn't take the mother out of the career woman or vice versa.

And you shouldn't have to, either.

PART I

ONE LIFE. ONE FAMILY.

When my oldest son was in elementary school, he wanted me to have lunch with him. I know lots of moms do this. So I set the date. I scheduled myself a free hour, plus driving time, so that I could do this for him.

The day arrived. I went to work early, got as much done as I could, then left and drove like a maniac to get back to our neighborhood by 11:10 a.m. I raced into the school and made it in time to line up with him for our meals. I asked him about his day, but he interrupted, anxious to point out the food I should choose and what I should avoid.

After paying, we picked up our trays, and I followed him to our assigned table. I sat down, cramming myself—suit and all—into a little chair next to his school buddies.

I knew who they were because they were the ones to whom he yelled, "This is my mom!" between bites.

I smiled and nodded at them when they yelled back either, "Really?" or "Cool!" I was feeling pretty good.

I had just picked up my plastic fork and glanced down at my chicken nuggets when the little boy across from us shot his hand into the air. And then another hand went up next to his. And another. A little girl down the way had her arm raised as well, her fingers wiggling for attention. It was then that I noticed that all of their trays had been reduced to a state of either rubble or rejection.

I looked at my son and discovered his hand was up, too. His tray was already empty.

I stared as the lunch coordinator nodded at them, and they all rose like popped kernels of corn to dump their trays and head out for recess.

"Thanks, Mom!" my son yelled as he headed out the door.

It had been less than seven minutes since I had walked in. I hadn't even opened my carton of milk.

The drive back to work that day was long. In my

head, I went over how hard I had worked to get there, wondering if that whirlwind interlude had been worth it. Had anything I'd done made a difference?

Truthfully, I don't even know if my son remembers that day, but I do. I remember all those moments when I decided to make my family more than a side note to my career, yet without giving up my career. Going to school that day was a lesson in living in the moment.

LAYERS

We all want to be successful at work and at home, but no one can maintain a perfect balance between the two. Regardless of what home is for us—a spouse and children, a domestic partner, a roommate, or our pets—we all have the desire to be the best at all of it. Yet the moment we think we have achieved balance, something falls out of place or doesn't happen in time and knocks everything else off kilter.

In either case, make your home life a priority. If your personal life is a mess, you'll never be your best at work. I firmly believe that to achieve success at work, you have to create a solid personal life. If problems at home are constantly nagging at your conscience, you will never be able to devote enough energy and talent to a successful career.

You really can't have success in one area of your life without having success in the others. It's all about creating alternatives, options, and backup plans, and it's about asking for help. You can't take the mother out of the career woman or the career out of the mother, so use both to your advantage.

Above all, try not to think of your life as a zero-sum game or as an equation that has to be balanced. I've learned there is not one magical answer to the question of "balance." Society tells us it's acceptable to succeed at work, provided it doesn't impact our home life. Unfortunately, trying to achieve this mythical "balance" simply causes us endless frustration. To minimize my frustration, I use the concept of "layers."

Think of it like layers of clothing. Wearing layers of clothing gives us options: We can add something if we need to, or we can take something away, allowing us to adapt to the changing weather. We wear more layers of clothing when it is cold, just like we need more layers of help when our work life is challenging. We wear fewer layers of clothing when it is warm and our work life is moving along more easily. And, sometimes, we bring an umbrella when we think it may rain, just like sometimes we need an umbrella to shelter ourselves professionally in the office.

Thinking in layers allows you to integrate your work and your personal time to create one life and one family.

Layer #1: Time Management

At an early age, I was introduced to the concept of time management. Each summer I had three jobs, and I had to make sure I could get to each one on time. Before I had a driver's license, that meant riding my bicycle or getting a ride from an older friend or my mom. Even after I could drive myself places, I had the added responsibility of making sure that my brother was where he was supposed to be. When the two of us were in high school, this included getting back and forth to sports and after-school activities. The free calendar from the local insurance company that hung on the wall in our kitchen was the time-management tool for my mom, my brother, and me.

Lists

We all have younger, more naïve versions of ourselves. Mine grappled with the idea that most lists were a waste of time. I believed that the time I spent making all those redundant lists would be better spent on doing the things I would be putting on the list. I justified this to myself by saying that I wouldn't forget anything that was important.

I definitely changed my mind, and I perfected my time-management skills out of necessity. My true appreciation for list-making came when I became VP of Product Management at Qwest Communications and my children were in elementary school. At work, I managed a large, growing team and had ever-expanding deliverables. At home, there were always field trips or away games to prepare for, bake sales to support, or parent-teacher conferences to attend. I was determined to be a good parent by staying involved while still accomplishing everything at the office. So I kept lists.

My process was to start with checklists in my head, categorize them, and then jot them down with the first pen and paper I could find. Also, when ink met the paper, my lists often fell into categories, such as grocery shopping, meal ideas, meeting agendas, and phone calls to make, among others.

My lists helped me kill the erroneous idea of multitasking. Instead of spreading myself too thin by working on multiple things at once, I focused on the big picture and broke it into small pieces.

I was also willing to crumple up my lists and start over. It wasn't about having twenty things to do; it was about having three or four. And those three or four would be scheduled, accomplished, and crossed off the list. Whenever the list began to overwhelm me, I knew it needed to be cut down to size. I always made my lists based on prioritizing what needed to get done next. Which item on my list was the wolf at the door?

Because so many things compete for my attention, I scribble thoughts and ideas in order to make lists of them. I do this out of necessity, and everyone who knows me makes fun of my ongoing scribbling, but I don't care. My lists allow me to be efficient and highly effective. They keep me on track and prevent me from getting overwhelmed.

Take the time to make lists, and make the time to complete the tasks on them.

Assign Time Limits for Everything You Do

Just how do you "make the time" to accomplish everything on your list that you set out to do? After all, the list is only effective if the items on it can be realistically completed. If you don't assign a time limit to completing each item, a list is just a paper mire—albeit one that reveals your priorities—without any proper results.

Begin by assigning a time limit for completing every item on your list.

Here's an example of how it works. If "wrap Christmas gifts" is on my list, in my head I allot forty minutes to get it done. I'm always aware of the time so as not to go over. After forty minutes is up, I need to be finished and on to the next item on my list. If I haven't finished wrapping, I stop anyway. I don't take another fifteen minutes for the sake of finishing. I have a hard stop, and I almost never go over the time allotted. If there is more wrapping to be done, I have to schedule more time to do it another day.

It's also a learning opportunity: Now I know that gift wrapping X number of gifts takes more than forty minutes, and I need either to schedule a larger block of time or to find some other solution to get the job done— like using gift bags and tissue paper next time.

The same is true at work. If I plan thirty minutes to work on a presentation, I don't spend extra time trying to make it perfect. I don't negotiate with myself! I think to myself, "This is the best I can do with the time that I've allotted." I'm not big on thesaurus searches or tinkering with color schemes, which means I'm a bit of a taskmaster with myself. I give 100 percent in the time allotted so that I can move on to the next task. I just can't afford to let the other items on my list slip.

Watch the Clock

If I have any sort of superpower, it's an awareness of time. I am always watching the clock. Wonder Woman had her bullet-deflecting bracelets. I have my wristwatch. My wristwatch tells me how much time *until* and how much time *since* for every meeting, errand, chore, and task I take on.

Without my watch I feel unprotected, and on more than one occasion I've run to the gift shop in the lobby or across the way to a Walgreens to purchase a spare cheap watch. I even have spares in my desk drawer, all for the purpose of not letting others rule my timetable. It's my way of never being held hostage if a meeting has passed its shelf life. And meetings do have a shelf life. Anything over an hour needs to be avoided like food gone bad.

Speaking of meetings—when you're running one, be focused. Don't pile on too much. Stick to the topic at hand. Only give relevant information. In the rare—and I stress rare—instance during a work meeting where an extra fifteen minutes is required to finish up, I always ask if everyone in the room has that extra fifteen minutes to spare. I respect the person who quietly slips out of a meeting unnoticed.

I have happily received the moniker of "time warden" from my peers because I am 100 percent comfortable with cutting someone off in order to keep the meeting on track. I use little checkpoints. Halfway through the meeting, I'll say something like, "Everyone, we have thirty minutes left." Then no one is shocked when I hammer it down with, "Okay, now we have ten minutes left." A final check of my wristwatch and a simple "I understand what you're saying, but we have to stop now" have deflected more long-winded meanderings than Wonder Woman's bracelets have deflected bullets, using the veil of time to cut someone off.

When I wasn't in control of the meetings, I was dealing with others who were, and bosses can be verbose. I've had more than one who was notorious for following streams of consciousness rather than schedules. If I sensed that my boss was stressed or not paying attention, I reprioritized my list of concerns to talk to him about, and I planned to come back to some things later and maybe, just maybe, to eliminate some items altogether.

That's it. Plan a meeting and execute it. And get a wristwatch.

Windows of Time

I didn't think of my workday as one concrete block of time that occurred during set hours, Monday through Friday. If I allowed it, work would keep me at the office long after my sons had gone to bed. I wanted to be home before their eyelids were droopy.

I wanted to eat with my family. I wanted to cook for them. So I did whatever was necessary to leave work at a reasonable hour and go home.

I knew that this couldn't be the end of my workday, but for that short period in the evening, I chiseled out a small chunk of time for my life outside of work. I wouldn't take a conference call or answer an email. My mantra was: *Two hours, for goodness' sake. It's not that big a deal in the grand scheme of things.*

At home, I gave my family my undivided attention.

While I prepared dinner, I would give my kids butter knives, and they would hack away at whatever vegetables we were having. They didn't have to be perfect; it was just an excuse to have them within arm's length. We had the normal family interactions with their normal ups and downs, but I was determined that I would not think of them as a chance for me to air grievances and get irritated. There were times when I did get upset and yelled, but I didn't want to be that *yelling* mom, that mom who let her kids have it over the dinner table because she was overly sensitive and exhausted from a stressful day at work.

I tried to consciously think: *I have a couple of hours to spend with my family. I don't want to be angry.*

After I had tucked the boys into bed, I would inevitably get my second wind. With the absence of incoming phone calls and real-time email exchanges at home, I was able to be more effective, often getting four hours of quality work completed in less than two.

Usually I did this work in front of the television with Pete sitting next to me. (Pete and my boys will tell you that I really don't watch TV; I just sit in front of it. However, when asked, I can recite the last two lines of the sitcom or pay-per-view movie.) Our dining room table in the center of the house became my workspace, as well as the spot where my sons, Jack and Joe, completed their school homework. This allowed all four of us to be in the same general area at the same time. Pete's and my bedroom was where Jack, Joe, and I practiced our speeches for presentations, meetings, or class projects. I also learned that during the early morning hours, before everyone else was awake, was my favorite time to work.

The fact is, there is never enough time in the day for everything you want to accomplish either at the office or at home. Either setting always has too much to do, which is one of the major contributors to feeling like you don't have "balance." I am suggesting that instead of worrying about finding "balance" between work and home, as if spending time on one necessarily drains time from the other, you think more simply. If you have a time-management technique that works for you at the office, bring it home as well. And while at home, don't feel bad about the time you're not spending with your family: Instead, use your time well to make the best of the time you do have and enjoy them.

Layer #2: One Calendar

In the beginning, I kept two separate calendars: one for work and one for home. I thought it was necessary to keep two very separate schedules in order to be in control of both facets of my life.

I wasn't working with any men who were open about what they were dealing with outside the office, so I followed their lead and never talked about my mothering dilemmas or about being a wife. I wanted to show a hard Teflon surface that would resonate with them and my boss. I didn't bring up my children. I would never have brought up the fact that I was having a problem with my son's teacher. What kind of weaknesses would I be exposing if I told them that an elementary school teacher was getting under my skin? Nor did I want to think about what might cross my boss's mind if he saw an entry for a second-grade Halloween party scrawled across my Tuesday morning calendar.

My calendar became a microcosm for what I felt I was battling in the rest of the world.

Keeping two calendars meant that I bifurcated my life, and as a consequence I felt bifurcated. This was not pleasant. Meeting and appointment overlaps occurred, and I dropped the ball and missed a few things because it was almost impossible to live without those overlaps.

But once I began to identify and hold sacred those hours outside the office, both to spend time with my husband and sons and, after dinner, to catch up or get ahead on projects, my original feelings of being overwhelmed and timid began to dissipate, and I became more productive. Because I was able to give 100 percent to whatever I was focused on—managing my blocks of time *without multitasking*—I was more effective at my job than I had ever been before.

Because I was able to give 100 percent to what-ever I was focused on—managing my blocks of time *without multitasking*—I was more effective at my job than I had ever been before.

I was becoming a better wife and mother in the process. It was a great confidence boost. The layers of time management were working!

The funny thing was that as I learned to use these layers in my work, I also craved eliminating other needless layers in my life. Maintaining two calendars was one such unnecessary layer, and so I stopped sawing myself in half and shucked the two calendars for one. I put everything personal and everything professional on one calendar and lived my life as one life.

As a consequence, I stopped feeling so segmented, and it felt increasingly comfortable to intertwine my two lives. At work, I mentioned my kids. I talked about my family. As I did this, my relationships improved at the office as well. I discovered that other people have family issues, too, and I became a mentor, someone people with families sought out for advice and perspective.

I realized that there wasn't a prejudice toward families at work; it was more of a sense of apathy. I realized my boss wasn't thinking less of me for having a family; he was just concentrating on my performance as an employee, as he should. As I became more and more industrious, he recognized and praised the projects I completed and every sales quota I met. And it wasn't as offensive that my boss took more than two years to learn my boys' names, since he began to be okay with me leaving work early to make a three o'clock appointment—even if that three o'clock appointment was my son's soccer game.

Layer #3: Weekends

While we all hope for a limited, forty-hour workweek, I have never had that luxury, and therefore I needed to create another layer—the weekend.

Work weekends. It's that plain, even if it's not simple.

We found that we had a huge advantage in Pete's fixed days and shifts. He volunteered to work Saturdays and Sundays so he could take care of the boys for three days during the week, which meant I would cover the weekends alone.

Saturday was my day to run errands with the boys in tow. I let the boys choose an inexpensive toy or treat as I pushed a cart through the stores. They bounced in the backseat as I picked up dry cleaning or dropped envelopes into the slot at the post office. We spent the day doing chores or going to soccer games.

I chose Saturday as my day to get priority household tasks out of the way because Sunday was my secret weapon.

Nobody likes to work on Sundays. This meant that on Sundays I had an empty office, a floor, and possibly the whole building at my disposal. I could take Jack and Joe in to work with me without disrupting anyone.

When my sons were little, I'd pack games, stickers, and dry erase markers, and they'd set up in the conference room adjacent to my office. In addition, in that wasteland of unoccupied offices, they were able to run freely down the halls. My idea was to keep them busy and content and myself productive.

I took them with me on those Sundays with the attitude that I would make it fun for them. I didn't know how much fun they were going to make it for me as well. For instance, when Joe was seven, after playing hide and seek under empty desks, he ran into my office to comment: "Hey, I thought you worked with people!

Where are they?" I laughed. It was like that. I learned to see my environment in new ways through their eyes.

I also learned to be prepared for the unexpected from our Sundays together. For example, it is very important to know that not all footballs are created equal. Some—the ones that are signed and sitting on pedestals—are not actually the kind one should tuck and run with, especially when the football didn't come from Mommy's office. (The football was returned, by the way, with none the wiser.)

And just like footballs, not all stickers are created alike. I had to have an embarrassing conversation with a coworker one Monday morning after the boys had covered his work printer with nonremovable stickers. Most people at my office were not familiar with the Pokémon characters. That morning they were exposed to Ash, Mew, Squirtle, and the whole group.

Sometimes, when things fell quiet, I wished I'd had theme music to warn me about what was coming next. One Sunday afternoon while in the conference room, Jack and Joe grew bored while filling the whiteboard with

Picasso-like expressions in blue, green, red, and black dry-erase markers. In search of loftier artistic pursuits, they extended the limits of their creativity to include the walls.

The wallpaper.

The wood trim.

The paint.

On the large conference table sat a clean, unused whiteboard eraser. Along with explaining its uses to them, I taught my boys how to scrub walls that day.

Layer #4: Child Care

The first big decision we make is whether or not we have children at all. I admire women who can honestly say that children are not for them. Once you decide that you do want children, the first panic is about the physical abuse your body will endure, and the second panic is about what you'll do for child care.

Day care failure. Three words that panic any working mother. What are we going to do when we both have to travel? What are we going to do when our child is sick and we both have important meetings? What are we going to do if . . .

We work to split ourselves off from our maternal feelings, and we theorize that if we have a system of day care for our children, with numerous backup and contingency plans, it will allow us to be at our workplace's beck and call, to meet every demand, and to run at any pace. Traditionally, a good day care plan has a minimum of three options: a friend, a coworker, or a relative. (In rare cases, I have called upon my secretary!) The more the better.

We also work on the belief that if we find the right people and create the right depth to our system, it will immunize us against feelings of guilt or inadequacy when it comes to our kids.

This belief is as readily available as office coffee. My first lesson about how wrong it can sometimes be was learned early and hard.

———

When Jack was still young enough to sit in his favorite swing but old enough to crawl, my original nanny gave notice, and I was forced to begin the search for a replacement.

I didn't have much success until a colleague suggested his daughter, an eager twenty-year-old who he said was wonderful with kids. Pete and I interviewed her. She said all the right things and had the right recommendations, so we hired her.

A few weeks passed and everything seemed to be fine, except that my son was developing an aversion to sitting in his swing. Whereas before, during his fussy time in the evening, he was soothed and comforted by the motion, now he arched his back and cried harder, as if its novelty had worn off.

I was also noticing that the nanny took longer than I thought was normal to answer my calls during the day, which, along with my son's behavior, was enough of a concern that I decided to investigate. One morning I went to work early, as usual, but after two hours, I mentioned to a coworker that I had left some important paperwork at home and that I needed to go and collect it.

It was a little white lie that seemed the perfect solution to bring me some peace of mind.

I was sure I was overreacting. Jack could have just outgrown his love for his swing, right? And wasn't it a *good* thing that the new nanny didn't answer the phone every time it rang?

On the drive home, one moment I was chiding myself about acting like a new mom, and the next I was working out the best way to steal quietly into the house.

My stealth plan was simple. I would pull the car into the driveway, slowly, and instead of announcing my arrival by the clanging of the garage door, I would slip in through the front entrance.

It worked perfectly. I was greeted by music, chatting, and the sound of running water coming from the kitchen. The nanny had no idea I had come home.

I didn't want to completely frighten her, but instead of the alarm I expected to see in her face, I saw horror as I entered the kitchen. I think her heart stopped. Mine did.

It was now ten o'clock in the morning, and the nanny had the phone tucked between her cheek and shoulder while she stood over the stove. Multiple pots and pans were bubbling and cooking, and every item in the pots or cut up on the counter was a dinner ingredient I'd purchased for an upcoming party that I was hosting for a group of women at my house.

The look on the girl's face would have been priceless had it not been my home and my child she was responsible for. She was literally caught with her mouth gaping midsentence, her hand frozen in midair. Then she started to shake.

There was no sign of my son.

"Where's Jack?" I asked.

"Uh, I don't know," she stammered.

Huh? I wondered if my ears were working as a wave of panic hit. "You don't *know*!" I yelped. I whirled around and tripped over my feet before regaining my balance. *Be okay! Be okay!* I thought as I rounded the wall.

I found him strapped into his swing, his closed eyelids crusty above his reddened cheeks. His chest heaved and faltered as he breathed. Even in sleep, he was still dealing with the length of time he had been left alone to cry.

I walked over to him and began popping open the straps to release him. *How could she have forgotten she'd put him in his swing?*

He woke up as I lifted the tray out of the way. He saw my face and smiled. My heart sank even further. I could see his whole little body now, and though he wasn't mortally wounded, he was still in his pajamas from the night before, his bottom distended by the filthy diaper he wore.

"Oh, my poor . . ."

The sound of my voice broke Jack out of his reverie, and his lips pulled down into a remembered pout. I scooped him up in my arms. He didn't have to cry anymore. I had him now and everything was going to be okay.

At this point, my vision turned red, and for the first time, I understood the all-consuming rage that was enough to remove appendages, limbs, and heads. I felt like a mother bear as I turned to go back into the kitchen. I don't remember the exact language I used when firing the nanny, but it was strong enough to send her running for the exit as I spun the heat dials to *off* on the stove.

As soon as the door closed behind her, I crumpled to the kitchen floor, Jack still in my arms.

What had I done? How could I have failed my son so thoroughly? I felt the sob build up in my chest, and I cried into his filthy PJs until he squirmed to get away—which reminded me that his diaper still needed to be changed.

I pulled myself to my feet and carried him into his shadowed bedroom. The blinds had never been raised to allow the morning light to come in. It matched my darkened mood.

I lay him down on the changing table and pulled off his pajamas. He twisted and squirmed, but I smiled down at him and handed him an extra diaper to pull apart as I cleaned him up and tossed his soiled diaper away. When he was cleaned up, I set him down at my feet and reached into a drawer to get out his clothes for the day. And then I caught my breath.

I had just fired the nanny. *I had just fired the nanny!*

It was now eleven in the morning, Pete was miles away at work, and I was already supposed to be back at the office!

I hefted Jack back into my arms and hurried into the kitchen. I needed to call work. I needed to call them and tell them . . .

I had no backup plan, and here I was at home, my half-naked son in my arms, with no options that would get me instantly to where I needed to be. I stared down at the numbers on the phone, and I realized that I had no idea what I was going to say.

What could I say?

I couldn't call my boss and say, "I fired the nanny this morning. Yes, *this* morning. Instead of being at my desk, where you think I am, I am at home, pretending to be stealth Mom because my son suddenly started to hate his swing, and I thought maybe the nanny wasn't answering my calls fast enough, and . . . and . . . and . . ."

I knew if I said any of that, I could kiss every promotion in my future good-bye.

I knew the unwritten code. People can have family emergencies, trips to the hospital, or car accidents, but the actual moment when a woman's career is instantly flushed down the toilet is the moment the words *day care* pass from her lips to the boss's ear.

Pete! I had to call Pete.

I took a cleansing breath that turned into a shudder and dialed. Pete answered, and I poured out my anger, frustration, and panic on the phone. He comforted my mixed bag of emotions.

"Call your mom," he suggested when I had finished.

I blinked back the tears.

"Call your mom and see if she can come out for a couple of days."

Yes, my Mom! It was like having life breathed back into me after drowning.

Thank heavens for that woman. She was on a plane from Wisconsin that night, and she agreed to take care of her grandson not just for two days but for *two weeks*, giving me a window in which I could find a more competent babysitter for my son.

At work, all anyone knew was that I had a family-excused absence that day. I showed up the next day feeling as if I had gone through battle, shell-shocked and jumpy, but at least I was back at work.

I have never forgotten the few seconds when the young woman to whom I had entrusted my son stared blankly at me and said she didn't know where he was—the fear, the terror, and the guilt of it. These same feelings can occur, of course, whether you're using a day care center, have an in-home day care provider, or take your child to a family member's home. And if I could cut those few seconds out of me, I would, but they're there: a constant reminder that no matter how professional I feel, in an instant I could be transformed back into my primary role. My son's mother.

The challenges haven't ended there. When one of my sons had difficulty learning to read, I was devastated, and the ever-ready mommy guilt rushed in. I felt horrible. In terms of child care, whenever there is a gap between our expectations and our performance, self-doubt pounces.

Or maybe we label it as a system failure instead. We question whether our efforts are good enough. We analyze. We hire and fire. And granted, there's sometimes a need for that. But is it the system, or is it something else?

A traditional workday is nine to five. Words like *multitasking* and *balance* are code words for the ability to run faster than an office mate or the ability to keep plates spinning in the air like the best Chinese juggler. Somehow we can keep everyone—be it at home or at the office—happy.

The problem with these concepts is that eventually one trips, or gravity wins.

> Words like *multitasking* and *balance* are code words for the ability to run faster than an office mate or the ability to keep plates spinning in the air like the best Chinese juggler. Somehow we can keep everyone— be it at home or at the office—happy. The problem with these concepts is that eventually one trips, or gravity wins.

Pete and I had approached our child care as if it were a tactical mission. We knew that we needed a third person, a nanny, to make it work, but besides that, Pete and I were willing to do whatever was necessary in order to get our work done without destroying our family or our peace of mind in the process.

I needed more than a normal forty-hour workweek to exceed expectations at my job. The system we designed was based on that need and other needs of ours rather than on some prescribed method we'd seen others create. We set up a flexible system of responsibilities for each of us. We got creative, and we were open to sacrificing time with one another and with friends in order to make it work.

But there is one universal truth: Even the best-laid plans can go awry. Pete could be called into work for emergencies any time of the day or night. If there was a lost hiker, missing person, or a forest fire, Pete was out the door. We could (and obviously did) have issues with nannies, or I could have an unexpected work trip.

I finally realized I needed to move away from the concept that layers of child care were what would grant me my desired results. While paying attention to the other layers of my overall strategy, I needed to expand those layers to encompass the real eight-hundred-pound gorilla in the room. I needed *layers to my work*.

Layer #5: Layers to Work

At the beginning of my career, I was promoted because I was good as an individual contributor: The more work I completed, the more work I was given. Success was rewarded with more work. Finally I received the promotion I was working so hard for. I became the director of new product development at US West, and I was responsible for a team of twenty with five direct reports. I was on top of the world; this was my big break. About six months into the job, I thought I was going to have to resign because I did not want the shame of being fired. I couldn't deliver anything on time or accurately, yet I was working harder than ever.

My problem was that I did not know how to delegate the work, lead through others, or say "no." Luckily, I had a boss who was willing to mentor me and who taught me that I needed to ask for help. My old style of doing it alone was not going to work. I could no longer stay up all night reworking someone else's work, and I had to make my peace with the fact that nobody was going to do it my way, but that was okay.

Turns out that maybe I didn't always have the best ideas. When I let go and trusted others, our team became one of the best performing teams and eventually led to my next promotion—to vice president.

———

There is not one answer or solution to the problem of "balance" that will make you feel like a good mother, wife, and friend. There is not one answer or solution that will suddenly make you perform better at work. But there are multiple techniques and multiple options, and thinking in layers will give you these alternatives. Take each day in pieces just like you do when you get dressed in the morning: choose your shoes, choose your jewelry, decide if you are going to put your hair up. You can't control everything that happens to you, but you can control how you react. Thinking in layers will allow you to integrate your work and your personal time to create one life and one family.

And one more point: It helps to find your rock, the thing you can count on if some of your layers become weak. For me, my husband, Pete, is the rock between my layers. Find your layers and find your rock, and then integrate them.

PART II

PUSH THROUGH ADVERSITY

I was born into an idyllic central Wisconsin community with farms as far as the eye could see.

My family started out pretty traditionally. It was the 1960s, and my father worked while my mother stayed home. My younger brother, Steve, and I were inseparable and only fifteen months apart in age. On the weekends, we would visit one set of grandparents or the other. I loved the weekends most when I got to play on the farm at my mother's parents' home.

During the summer, our family always took a camping trip.

Later, I was captain of the cheerleading squad, an honor student, and girlfriend of one of the popular boys in school.

As a senior, I was also voted *Most Likely to Succeed* by my graduating class.

These honors, along with my rise in the corporate world, would seem to cast me in a favored, golden light. But although those titles and labels had something to do with my accomplishments, in many ways, they were like using a Band-Aid to close an open chest wound.

The cheerleading hands that I used to lift the lightest of us to the top of the pyramid on the football field were the same hands I used in my after-school job to sort and file papers, a position the federal government provided to low-income kids. The bright eyes of my mother that had followed me as a child were now dulled under the weight of a divorce and her return to work in an initially unsuccessful battle to make ends meet.

The hours I spent getting the best grades were also spent in helping my younger brother do his homework, in doing the shopping, and in making dinner. At a very young age, my willpower was tested by mental illness, divorce, and suicide.

I've never hidden from these experiences, nor do I wallow in them. These achievements and difficulties have simply shaped who I am.

You can't control the circumstances that happen to you, or the setbacks, but you can control how you react to them. You can decide if negative occurrences are going to impact your future. None of these betweentimes would ever be called golden, but these are the factors that created my drive and stamina. If you are determined, focused, and creative, positive energy will come your way. Everyone has a story, but you are the one who determines that story's ending. I am sharing a few of my stories in the hope you will be inspired to push through your adversity, small or large.

GROWING UP FAST— MENTAL ILLNESS, DIVORCE, SUICIDE

Delafield, Wisconsin, was an ideal place to grow up.

The families on our street got together nearly every weekend for some milestone to mark and to celebrate, whether it was a birthday, a baptism, or the start of spring. We had block parties in the summer, and in the fall and winter were hunting and fishing trips to take. I remember a lot of laughter, and there were games, not only for the kids but for the parents, too. I still remember watching adult chins grappling with Pass the Orange or cringing as they played Twister. As a young person, I was taught that every day can be a party, and I reached back to those good memories as I raised my children, and reach back to those memories even now.

My mother was full of life then. She had started her married life as a traditional stay-at-home mom, and my father, who had served in the United States Navy, had translated his skills from the service into a civilian position at a large hospital in Milwaukee. He was a purchasing agent, and he commuted back and forth. Life was good. But it wasn't to last.

When I was eight, the cracks began to show in our idyllic life. My grandmother, my father's mother, had committed suicide, and the loss seemed to trigger something dark in him. The man I knew to have a quiet demeanor became agitated. His pensive moods would break open like a thunderclap over our heads, and he would rage.

In the beginning, that rage was as far as it went. But as he began to drink more and more heavily, the violence escalated, until his abuse turned into physical attacks on my mother.

She was aware of the effect my father's deterioration

was having on my younger brother and me, and she did the best she could to shield us, but trying to protect us was all she could do. This was the hard way to learn about mental illness.

As my father's behavior became more erratic and violent, it affected not just our home, but it tipped the balance for him at work as well, and he was eventually fired. He was in and out of hospitals and on and off of medications. He didn't improve with treatment, and my brother and I were left to grasp at the pointlessness of the situation.

Our next-door neighbors, Ann and Dick Thome, were the youngest couple on our block. On the worst nights, my mother would often push us out the door, and we knew to cross our driveway to the Thomes'. Their door was open, and they were always waiting. Although they were raising their own children, they fit us into their lives.

The constant upheaval could not continue. And it didn't. Eventually my father disappeared. My mother was suddenly alone and left to face a future very different from the one she had imagined when she had married her high school sweetheart at eighteen. She was now thirty years old, and she had to start a career in order to support her family.

She had a plan that unfolded over that year. First, she took any small jobs—from waitressing to housecleaning—to pay the bills. She decided she needed to go back to school, and started attending college in the evening. Steve and I turned into our street's only latchkey kids. This did not go unnoticed by the neighbors. They all pitched in to help the new single mom, especially the Thomes, who embraced us as their adopted older kids. Ann taught me how to sew and cook, and Dick taught my brother how to hunt and fish. They took on the active role of our parents and were my mom's eyes and ears.

About this time is when I met Robin and her family. It was sixth grade, and soon I was hanging out at Robin's house as often as I was at the Thomes'. I began to blend into her family as if I was just another one of their kids.

One afternoon I went grocery shopping with Robin and her mother. As we filled up the belt of the checkout line, I began sorting the groceries just as I did when I shopped with my mother. I separated the food we paid for with cash from the food we paid for with "stamps." After a minute, Robin asked me why I was doing that. I answered by asking her why she *wasn't* doing that. Her mother knew exactly what was going on, and she nicely said, "Thank you for helping me, Teresa. We can just put it all together." Later, when I went home, my mother explained to me what welfare and food stamps were all about.

Many years later, I was in the grocery store with my children. They observed a similar situation and asked me why the person was sorting and paying differently than we were. It gave me the opportunity to explain how fortunate we were and how it wasn't always that way when I had grown up with their Grandma Mary. They were also at the age where I could explain our political system and the concept of taking care of others. When I look back on it now, I think that growing up with these experiences is why I continue to be so involved in charities and volunteering. I also took a strong role in making sure that the company I worked for gave back to communities and individuals. Almost everyone needs help at some point in his or her life.

A turning point for me was when I reached sixteen. My mother's schedule was getting more and more demanding with work and school. Both were going very well for her, but it meant that she was home less and less. When I passed my driver's test, she handed me the keys to the car and said, "Take care of your brother." I groaned inside. I knew she didn't have another choice, but I wasn't thrilled with what this would mean for me. I was now the one primarily responsible for cleaning the house, doing the laundry and the cooking, and caring for my younger brother. It was the cold metal of the keys becoming warm in my hand that finally made me look up into my mother's face. And there it was. The hope and pride evident in her smile. She believed me capable. She knew that I could do it, and she was right, but suddenly to be responsible for another person was not what a sixteen-year-old wants. I looked back down at the keys, feeling their weight. She hadn't had much choice when my father left. Who was I to complain now?

I kept up appearances, but my brother and I both became more and more aware of her continued absence, and we became very independent.

We intermingled a lot because we were so close in age. He talked to me a lot about his relationships and friends. I knew about his girlfriends and whether he was dumping one or going out with someone new. We had our disagreements, but we had found the unity that comes with needing to rely on one another. My brother had an amazing heart, and he was incredibly entertaining.

Still, when I left for college, I couldn't pack fast enough. The responsibilities that intimidated new college freshman weren't daunting for me. They were exhilarating. It was me against the world. It was an exciting fresh start. But as I drove away from the house, I looked behind me and felt something flutter in my stomach.

College was a blast. I loved the constant activity— always something to do with somebody. I felt like there was someone new to meet behind every corner, and everyone around those corners was friendly. Since school came easy to me, it was a time in my life when I could ask myself what was the biggest worry I had, and when I could answer: "Oh yeah, a test. What's the big deal?" I didn't feel overwhelmed. I never felt I was dying under the pressure. I just loved the open learning atmosphere— and I loved to go to the parties, too.

I met Pete early in my freshman year. It was at our dorm orientation social. Everyone was sitting in a circle around the room, including a handful of sophomores who were there to help the new freshmen. We began introducing ourselves, and Pete immediately captivated me. Our relationship developed enough that I brought him home the Christmas of my freshman year to "meet the family."

While I had a growing love for my new boyfriend, things at home were different when I returned for that first summer break. It was true that my brother didn't need me so much when he got his own driver's license, but I felt a distance growing between us that seemed greater than the lack of our driving time together warranted. I also noticed that he had gotten a new group of friends.

They were not the jocks he used to be with; these new friends were the troubled kids, the ones who partied too hard and who were experimenting with pot and cocaine. He started coming home even less than before, and when he was home, he spent most of his time sleeping. I didn't have the sophistication to see that these changes were a sign of something possibly worse.

I had been back at school for only a couple of weeks when I got a knock on my dorm door at 3:00 a.m. on January 18, 1983. Dick Thome was standing in my doorway, looking stricken. I felt chilled, and my stomach clenched. All I could think was: *What has happened to Ann? Or their kids? Is someone hurt?* Logically, it didn't make any sense that Dick would have driven four hours away from his home to tell me that something was wrong with *his* family, but you don't always think things out clearly at three in the morning.

At around three in the afternoon on January 17, the day before, my brother Steve had taken his life, using the exhaust fumes from his car. No adequate words can describe how this made me feel.

Suicide has many cutting edges. The feeling of missing him, of being robbed of having him in my life, cuts so deeply. And another slash is that there is nobody to complain to about the injustice of his being gone. The unanswered questions cut the deepest, though. Why does an eighteen-year-old commit suicide? I have to wonder: Why then? Why that day? What was the impetus? What was so bad that had made him say on that Tuesday afternoon: "This is the end"? How is it a kid that looks good on the surface, does well in school, has dates, seems to be a normal high school kid, how is it that he . . . There hadn't even been a cry for help. He left no note, but even if he had left one, how can anyone understand definitively why a person chooses to take such a drastic step? The questions are endless and are guaranteed to be left behind in the wake of a suicide.

Also left behind were the wounds and regrets of those who were closest to him. Our collective grief was still raw when the police added their own blow. Based on evidence they pulled from the scene, they told us that Steve might have wanted to change his mind. It appeared that he had tried to lift our garage door to let out the exhaust. But he had waited too long, and he was too weak to lift it on its rusted and broken hinges.

I didn't know any of that when Dick was standing in my doorway. All I knew was that pain was visible on his usual stoic face. The man who had served in Vietnam as a US Marine was bursting into tears. He had driven the long, cold four hours to my school, argued with and stood fast against the security guards who wanted to know why he was there to get me at such an ungodly hour, and all so that someone was there in person to tell me what had happened to Steve. I stood frozen as he got himself under control enough to choke out the words to tell me that my baby brother was . . .

I arrived home early the next morning with Pete and Dick, when the sun was just beginning to warm the ice that crusted the pavement outside my house, and I saw the police tape across my driveway. I was in shock, but more distressing was finding my mother immobilized with grief inside the house. She had tragically lost her son and was barely responsive.

Decisions had to be made, and as the morning and afternoon progressed, my mother needed to act, yet she didn't make a move. Suddenly I was the one at the center of the activity. Scores of questions came at me, and in that vacuum with nobody else to turn to, I began to make decisions. They weren't profound or above an almost automatic response mode, but they were enough. Robotic and almost silent, I moved through a growing list of items.

> Scores of questions came at me, and in that vacuum with nobody else to turn to, I began to make decisions. They weren't profound . . . but they were enough.

I was only nineteen, and along with Pete, I had to decide what kind of casket to choose for my brother. We did. We picked out his casket. I arranged the funeral, which will always be hazy. The whole thing turned into a blur of days, a cloudiness of stuff. But there are moments that I can remember clearly. I had to go with the police to Steve's school and clean out his lockers. They were still looking for the clues, as we all were. Everyone was looking for a note, an explanation, a reason for his passing, but we never found anything. No one did.

I also saw my father. I hadn't seen him in seven or eight years. He showed up for the funeral. His sisters, my aunts, must have called him. He sat alone on the other side of the room, looking heavily medicated. After the funeral, he wandered off again. He never spoke to me. I didn't talk to him, either.

With the hazy grief that clouded around those few days, I carried away with me one memory that had a lasting effect. It was of Pete sobbing beside me while we sat in Steve's bedroom. To this day, this has been the only time I've seen him cry like that, and it still means so much to me that he knew my brother and that he grieved. Without clear answers as to why this all had happened, I came to rest on the idea that while I could handle early independence, maybe Steve could not. He had just gotten lost somewhere along the way and hadn't known how to get himself out, just as he hadn't had the strength to lift the garage door by himself. I was exhausted, but I didn't know what else to do but to keep going. I didn't want to slow down. I threw myself into school and work.

All this work made me feel as if I had slogged through the worst of my anger and frustration. That is, until my own children were born and started growing up. Then I felt something break open inside of me. It was strange: I felt a rush of emotions that I hadn't realized I had shut out. It was exhilarating and disturbing at the same time. I realized that being a mother was forcing me to see what had happened with Steve differently. I was floored to realize that I was still angry at what had happened. Now the questions changed from questions of why to questions of what if. What if my father had never left? What if my mother had not been so busy with work and school? What if I had chosen a college closer to home? I wanted to question everyone's motivation and to hold people accountable. I struggled with these feelings. I hated carrying around angry thoughts and wanting to lay blame. After all these years, why now?

Why? Because.

Added to this, I recognized how I now looked at Pete differently. I had been guarded and survival-like up to that point; I had not been as giving with Pete, even after we were married. I look back and see how cautious I was. *After all, if you don't let anyone get too close, they can't hurt you or leave you.* I didn't want these things competing for space inside of me.

So I didn't.

I took stock of everything that had happened to me. What I realized was that instead of wallowing in what had happened, I would rather identify pitfalls to avoid. I was determined to put extra effort into not repeating the mistakes I felt on some level that I and others had made in the past.

This had the greatest impact on how I chose to raise my boys. Anytime when I felt wary of a situation or I felt like I was in a pinch, I chose my family first. That's why

I didn't chase my career and run myself and my family out of Denver. I would have taken a lesser job in order to keep them stable. I refused to disrupt my children's lives. Based on my experiences, there was no way I was going to take a chance.

INFERTILITY

Getting my two boys onto this earth was a Herculean experience. Early on in our marriage, Pete and I planned for children, as most couples do. I was intense about it from the beginning. I analyzed and planned and prepared for motherhood like it was an extension or a facet of my job. When the appropriate time came, Pete and I happily ditched the birth control and began "trying." It's the damnedest thing when you want to get pregnant and you don't. I didn't sweat after the first three months when nothing happened. Nor throughout the rest of the first year.

The second year began to worry me a bit. I had heard that sometimes it just takes a while, and I told myself to relax, but there is a horrible feeling of inadequacy when you can't contribute what you always took for granted that you could—or should. I am the woman. It is my job to carry the baby and, like all my jobs, I wanted to do it well. It was a tangible sadness laced with lots of "Why me?"—or, rather, "Why not me?" I felt worthless. I began researching infertility issues to find clues. I started by casually talking to friends, but then I called and made my first appointment with a doctor.

It didn't bother me that other couples we knew had children already or were pregnant. I wasn't that kind of jealous. What bothered me were the questions. I didn't want to have to explain to everyone who asked why we didn't have children yet. I didn't want to have to talk about such a painful subject each time it came up. I wanted to avoid the whole thing. It is dreadful when you can't avoid it.

I had started out with a regular obstetrician, but now I went looking for the best fertility specialists. I peed on sticks, gave blood, and faithfully allowed examinations. I answered every charted question. I was a human guinea pig. Most individuals who have IVs, shots, and bodily fluids analyzed are there involuntarily in order to cure or prevent something. I was asking for the opposite, and it felt as bizarre as it sounds. This was a special kind of hell.

Pete was amazing and supportive. When doctors could not initially find anything wrong with me, he agreed to being poked and prodded as I had been. Shortly, he was given a clean bill of health and the attention turned back to me again. But with each new test, and each cure suggested, the lack of success began to wear me thin. The entire process was humiliating, and I felt trapped in a crazy cycle. Flying alongside was Pete, my wingman.

I went to one appointment where a doctor actually said, "You know, Teresa, sometimes we can't find a physical reason for what is happening. Sometimes there are other factors." My ears perked up. That sounded encouraging.

"Sometimes"—he held my gaze and spoke slowly, making sure I was listening—"you might just need to relax and let things happen naturally."

I walked out of that appointment feeling spent. This was a new low point. Could he be right? Maybe I wasn't relaxed. After months and months of disappointment and tests, how could I not be a little tense? I kept telling myself that it had to be possible. That I could win.

An emergency drew my regular doctor away and he was replaced. Enter Dr. Janet Dean. The appointment with this new, young female doctor who was just starting her practice began as usual, until she asked a pivotal question: "Has anyone ever talked to you about having a laparoscopy to check things out?"

I dropped my chin and shook my head no.

"Hmmm," she said. "To me, what you're describing sounds a lot like a case of endometriosis. The only way to get a proper diagnosis, however, is through a laparoscopy. If my suspicions are correct and endometriosis is what we're dealing with, then the surgery will determine the severity of your case and will also give us an idea if this is the cause of your not getting pregnant." She clicked her tongue as she reached over and began to add another note to my chart. "If you're game, I would like to schedule your surgery as soon as possible."

A few days later, it was confirmed that the reason for

my not getting pregnant was not related to tension but to an aggressive case of stage 4 endometriosis, which meant that endometrial cells had overgrown my ovaries and fallopian tubes and were running rampant in my body. Dr. Dean informed us that even after we removed the endometriosis, my chances of becoming pregnant were low. For the first time, Pete and I were faced with the fact that we may never have our own children. We discussed all of the alternatives, from adopting a child to having a surrogate mother. I underwent the surgery to remove the lesions. It was painful, and I was away from work for six weeks in order to recover.

At that time, I worked for a man who really did not want to hear about things like this. He couldn't even look at me and just wanted to know when I was coming back. For the first time in my career, I didn't care if I ever went back. Nothing was more important to me than recovering and defeating the odds I had been given. I also studied the disease as much as I could, even though there was not much information publicly available. I joined the National Endometriosis Association, headquartered in

Milwaukee, Wisconsin, which provided another lesson in the power of associations and support groups, as well as in the importance of funding research.

Within the year, I became pregnant with Jack and had a wonderful, healthy pregnancy. He was induced ten days late and kicked and screamed the whole way, but it was worth it.

The tragedy of endometriosis is that it grows back. When Pete and I wanted to have another child, I went in for another round of surgeries and hormones. Joe was then conceived—our second little miracle.

Once again, however, the endometriosis grew back, and my only solution was a hysterectomy. That decision was almost as emotional as the beginning of this journey. The thought of never being able to have another child was devastating, even though Pete and I had decided we only wanted the two. I felt like a part of being a woman was stripped away. The only good news was that I wouldn't be sick anymore—and no more periods!

SEPTEMBER MELTDOWNS—COWBOY[GIRL] UP

Adversity comes in all sizes and shapes and happens both at home and at work. An old saying by writer Charles Swindoll goes: "Life is 10 percent what happens to you and 90 percent how you react to it." Or, in the words of Winston Churchill: "Attitude is a little thing that makes a big difference." We are in charge of our attitudes. We can't dictate what happens to us, but we can determine how we will react to those events that can be viewed as setbacks. But everyone has bad days.

And some of us have a whole bad month. *Annually.*

Once a year, like clockwork, I failed at keeping it together. Everyone feels discouraged and has a meltdown once in a while. But mine, as my best friend pointed out, seemed to happen on an epic scale and to occur around the same time every year. These came to be known unaffectionately as my "September Meltdowns."

At this time of the year, my two worlds collided. At work, we were always behind in our financial commitments, and in order to get the fourth quarter in line, we would need to make expense cuts. The pressure was unbelievable and unpleasant. Meanwhile, the kids going back to school meant a busy coordination of school, sports, and activities. As the leaves began changing on the trees, it was harder for me to get up in the morning. I did get up, but I felt like I had to push a big rig up the side of a mountain in order to do it. Everything felt insurmountable during this time, and I started grumbling around the house. "The dishes go in the dishwasher." "Why do the boys leave their stuff in the kitchen?" "Can't you pick up your clothes and shoes?" (These last two were directed at Pete.) I didn't hide away in my room. I wanted everyone else to go down with me. *We should all be miserable together.*

These were the symptoms that showed that "the

meltdown" had arrived. After the grumbling, the crying kicked off. Give me something that would normally have been okay and I would crumple into tears. Big tears. Giant red runny nose. Sniffles that emphasized how stuffed up I was and gasping that could be heard across the street. (Did I mention that everything about my meltdowns was exaggerated?) These emotional outbreaks lasted thirty minutes straight. By the time they were over, my eyes had puffed up and I was exhausted.

There were times when I was able to keep this from the kids; naturally, this made them upset. Pete was great at ushering the boys away from my weeping and wailing storms. As they got older, though, exposure to them became unavoidable, and everyone bore witness to my dramatics. I was something to behold. When Pete could get me to a restaurant, I just didn't feel like eating. Nothing sounded good. The things that I normally loved didn't bring me any joy. Only a drink sounded good. A margarita, perhaps? Maybe three?

Of course, the meltdowns would go with me to work. I was just short-tempered and agitated all around. How was I supposed to figure out how to reduce my budget by millions of dollars? Why did we have to go through this every year? From my compromised perspective, there was no believing that the sun would ever shine on me again.

Thank God for Pete. He would live through a few days of this, be comforting, shield the children, and even run for more tequila if I needed it. But eventually, he would call "time." He had a phrase he used to announce that I was finished. He would saunter into whatever room I was polluting with my meltdown, lean against the wall, and say in the way only Pete can say it: "Teresa. Cowboy up."

At the end of the day—or at least every time September came around—all over again I learned a valuable lesson about adversity, setbacks, disappointments, difficulties, and everything else that seemed to come rolling down the pike. Sometimes it's just a matter of "cowboying up" and pushing through. It takes faith that things will work out. They always do, and it helps that Pete has an uncanny ability to set my mind right again.

WEARING THE GAME FACE—CRY OR THROW UP?

I have always had to deal with managing the pressures I feel from work. I owned the process in order to deliver results. When I was the chief operating officer (COO), I knew every decision mattered. Each decision had far greater scope than the immediate situation sometimes indicated. At this time in my career, my decisions— including an impending merger of my company—were guaranteed to impact every one of the thirty thousand employees under my management. No pressure at all.

This is why I treated people the way I did. I knew that every employee was vital to the company, and I approached everyone as I wished to be treated. I didn't think I was better than someone else because of a title. I could walk onto any floor and talk to anybody because I knew their concerns were the same as mine.

That also meant that I had the same human reactions to stress as everyone else, but I always tried to keep my game face on. Why? Because when you are in a leadership role, that is what people expect of you. Nobody wants to go home from work and tell their family: "Guess what? I saw my boss have a complete meltdown today and break into tears!"

The women's bathroom is a great getaway. On the floor that I was on, my chances of running into another woman were almost zero percent. So that was my escape. I could break into tears, wash my face, dry off, touch up my makeup, and nobody was the wiser. In one particular case, I was having difficulty pulling it together. Noting how long I'd been gone, my secretary came into the bathroom to check on me. (She *always* knew what I was up to.) She said, "They're all waiting in your office to begin the meeting. What should I tell them?" I said, "I don't know . . . Tell them I'm on an important call in another office and that I'll be there in five minutes."

"Will do. Oh—don't forget to touch up your mascara!" We were a team, and we started affectionately calling the women's bathroom the "cry room."

It turns out I wasn't the only one who made that trek. Other women executives and their secretaries found our secret. Funny thing was, once we started sharing stories about the stress we felt, we could laugh about it. The women's bathroom became a private meeting room bursting with tears and laughter at the same time. We started keeping supplies—lotion, hairspray, curling iron, and so forth—in the bathroom that we could all use.

When I was named COO of Qwest, it was unexpected, and the decision was made urgently because the previous COO had departed abruptly. Therefore, my immediate task was to travel to our major shareholders and institutional investors to reassure them the company was fine and that I was the right choice. This was new territory for me; my previous interaction with Wall Street had been limited. Two others from Qwest joined me for the journey to the East Coast, and our schedules were very tight, with a typical day involving a run from

Fidelity to Oppenheimer to Citibank to Blackrock, to name a few. Up the elevator, talk fast, down the elevator, up the elevator, talk fast, down the elevator. Three Diet Cokes, two cookies, and on to the next meeting.

When I finally collapsed in my hotel room, I honestly thought I could not get up again. What was I doing? What did I say? How did I get here? Was the stock going to decline? What would they write about me? I vomited, set my alarm for the morning—in case I slept—and prayed for time to pass.

My alarm didn't have to go off because I didn't sleep. When morning came, I looked at myself in the mirror and thought, "I can't do this again!" I looked awful, and I hadn't brought enough makeup to cover up everything. I vomited again, and then I got dressed and put on my game face.

We did the whole routine again before flying back to Denver. The trip was a success, and the two men I was with were extremely supportive, grateful, and encouraging.

Why am I sharing these episodes from my life with you? Well, why not? I have had more than one person approach me in recent years with the belief that my life has been easier than most people's lives, as if my past was somehow void of adversity or pain. There was an assumption that I had arrived at the pinnacle of my career while at the same time managing my family because somehow I had been able to avoid any discomfort. If there had been discomfort—according to this assumption, which I heard too often—I would have given up.

I hope you see that this is so detrimental to every woman who is striving to accomplish more in her life. Likewise, it's an insult to men who care for their families as much as their careers. The most offensive people make this assumption because it gives them an explanation, an excuse, all ready for them when they fail. They can say, "I can't be as successful as her because she wasn't born with all the problems that I was born with. She doesn't know any of the struggles I faced." And it's discouraging to those who are looking for someone who can say, "Yes, it's hard, but it can be done!"

There was a time when I would not have shared these stories because I thought they revealed weakness. Now I realize that sharing is the best thing anyone can do. Sharing creates laughter and brings new ideas to light. What's more, it turns out that many have had the same feelings and experiences—and if you have, know that you're not alone.

We all have our stories of facing adversity. You determine the ending.

PART III

THE PRIVILEGES OF LEADERSHIP

I considered my job at Qwest to be more than just the work I did. My company was part of my family. I felt responsible to the people in it. As I rose in the levels of the company and my decisions took on a greater scope, the pressure increased. I felt that the work came with strings attached—strings that paid higher salaries but also created a weight of responsibility I couldn't ignore. As my promotions continued, I became more accountable for all my actions. The decisions I made would impact my team either positively or negatively, depending on how well I could see around corners. Each assignment had its own unique challenges, and I could not have accomplished all that I did without the help and input from those around me. I never took for granted the privilege of being part of a greater whole. And so I approached each new assignment with a ferocious appetite to succeed, knowing that people were counting on me. What I did mattered.

THE INTANGIBLES OF REPRESENTING A MULTITUDE

Union Negotiations

The most daunting task in my professional career happened during a period when my company was reeling from a blackened reputation as a result of the scandal of our previous CEO being indicted. The new CEO faced the challenges of correcting the missteps of his predecessor and addressing the needs of the recovery.

One of the most glaring issues was the need to open a collective bargaining process with the Communication Workers of America, the union that represented 65 percent of Qwest employees. The former CEO had not allowed that bargaining process to occur, and the union was demanding that issues in the soon-to-expire contract be addressed.

Negotiating with a union isn't easy even during the best of times, but now, because of the financial constraints, the outcome of negotiations could determine the company's very survival. I was glad that one of my peers was going to be the one to deal with it—or so I thought.

I was happily sitting in the conference room having a monthly operational review meeting with my staff when the CEO's assistant came to get me.

"Dick needs to see you," she said with a smile.

I checked my watch, slightly annoyed. *Couldn't it wait?* She raised her eyebrows and shoulders at the same time, seemingly reading my mind. *Okay.* I nodded.

Dick greeted me in his office with a nod and motioned for me to take a seat in the chair on the other side of his desk.

"So, here's what I want," he began. "I need you to lead the negotiations with the union. That also means you'll be head of HR, but don't worry about all of that. Just focus on the union contract. Starting immediately." He lifted his chin in the direction of my interrupted meeting down the hall. "Let me know who on your team can take over for you."

Stunned, I sat in the chair for a few more seconds, trying to digest what had just happened. I knew nothing about unions, pensions, health care, benefits, or any such thing. I was all about sales and operations, *not* human resources. To put me in charge of this contract negotiation was insane. He obviously had not thought this through.

I calmly explained to him my lack of experience in this field or in anything HR related. "There has to be someone else who would be better at this," I pleaded.

He was shaking his head. I knew he had listened, but I had the first tingle of a sinking feeling that I was going to lose this argument. He cleared his throat. "Teresa, I know why you're hesitating. But sending in an operational person like you is the easiest way to get this done." He gazed hard at me. "You are, in fact, the only one who I can send to do this. You know the company. You know the culture. You know the people. We need to get this done, and we need to get it done right." He sighed, waving as if dismissing me. "But by all means, take a look at the old contract. Ask around. Get a feel for what I'm asking you to do."

I felt my mouth open and close again. I wasn't going to be able to fight my way out of this. And it was true that he was right. A new person would never be able to come in and replicate my experience with the company. No one in HR had my operational experience.

I *had* been there for fifteen years.

I *did* know the company, the culture, and the people. I knew the rhythm of it all. For instance, I knew how the call centers and the field people worked within their division, and I knew how each division worked together. At some point during my tenure, most of these people had reported to me. I understood the big picture.

My shoulders sagged.

The worst thing was this: Dick knew my reputation as someone who had never given up, even when I'd been thrown into the fire.

I hated that he was going to win.

I nodded and headed back to the conference room where my team was waiting, my mind reeling.

By the end of the day, I could feel the proverbial flames licking at my heels. I had a ream of paper on my desk and an understanding that this collective bargaining process was not only going to hurt, but that it was also long overdue.

The union was right in thinking they had a lot to talk about due to the number of years that had passed. During the preceding years, during extensions, they had helped the company tremendously. Now, as the company tried to right its footing in order to step out again, the union wanted to be in a better position.

Going to negotiations at the union table meant negotiating every conceivable facet of the company's work rules, the rules that controlled how Qwest employees could conduct business with every single one of our customers on a day-to-day basis. It would define the company, really, and it would determine how we synthesized as a company by tackling pay, benefits, and a mountain of work-life issues.

I felt like there was a two-ton elephant I was being asked to eat: a very big, angry, rampaging elephant that didn't want to be eaten.

Emotional

One of my first tasks was to fly to Phoenix, Arizona, to meet with the local union leadership. Although this local was the most powerful and reputed to be the most difficult, I had dealt with many unhappy customers, employees, and vendors, so this did not seem like it would be too hard.

I walked in almost cheerfully, but quickly came to a halt. I don't know what I had expected, but it wasn't this. The union had arrived in full force. I brought one person with me, and they had brought eight—something I would later learn was to be the norm.

I was startled by the variety of clothing they wore, but most shocking was the woman who I initially thought was having a wardrobe malfunction. In reality, she was intentionally exposing enough of her breasts so that everyone could clearly see the union's initials, CWA, tattooed across her chest.

Now that was devotion. I reached into my bag. The most I had on me was a pen with the Qwest logo on it.

Nevertheless, I smiled and took a seat at the head of the table, feeling like I had entered a rowdy version of a TV court show rather than a business meeting. This was the first of many unique experiences I was about to have.

When the official day came to begin the formal collective bargaining negotiations, I walked into a small, stuffy room and glanced at the contract that lay in front of me. It was the size of a book, and it taunted me with its legalese. One of the lawyers in the room leaned over my shoulder and told me it was time to start. I glanced at the large clock on the wall and at the stenographer. It was up to me to open the negotiating table, and I turned to the sea of flushed faces. They were filled with the pinks and reds of defiance and anticipation.

I was ready to begin, but they were all glaring at me. Who was I supposed to address? I swallowed down the nervous idea that I could start with something like, "Isn't it a beautiful day?" Knowing that wasn't the right tone, I read the speech that someone slipped under my hand at the last moment.

I've since forgotten the speech.

And so it began, the beginning of a tremendous number of difficult lessons I was to learn. It was the beginning of having all of my corporate assumptions challenged, and it was incredibly uncomfortable.

For six months, we worked day and night. Sometimes my team and I worked alone, strategizing and creating proposals. On other days, we bargained officially, and then there were the meetings "on the side" or "off table." My patience had met its match, but we were all there for the same reason, right?

I needed to change perspectives, so I acted like the union was the customer, and I treated them with the same respect and appreciation a customer deserved. I treated the negotiations like a sale I was trying to win.

But it wasn't going to be that easy.

Seek Outside Input

Even though we had what looked like all the time in the world, with the battleground mind-set evident in our meetings, I feared the deadline would come and go without an agreement. We would fail. And I saw no way to stave off the strike that would happen as a consequence—a strike that would happen if *I* didn't perform, if *I* didn't manage to make a breakthrough.

I just did not understand the negotiating system— the seeming lack of progress, and the constant flow of intimidating people the union brought to every meeting. It seemed to have been set up for the sole purpose of being difficult, of making the negotiations difficult for difficulty's sake. So I asked for help.

"It's a process. You just have to get through it," Dick said as preamble to explaining the value of a well-negotiated and binding agreement to me. He had many years of experience with the union, and he could accurately articulate many of the views the union members held. He leaned back in his chair. "The process keeps everybody honest."

"But I don't expect anyone to work harder than I do. Just to work until the job's done."

Dick just looked over the top of his glasses at me.

"It's like they think I'm trying to take advantage of them."

Still nothing.

"I'm not!" I burst out.

Dick shook his head. "Teresa, I'm not saying *you* would take advantage of them. But not everyone is *you*."

Ah, that was true.

"Think of it as something that protects you and the company as well. Again, it keeps everybody honest. You and them."

"But they're so hostile," I hissed. Here Dick couldn't help his mouth from pulling tight into a frown. He had seen me angry that day, and it was lucky that no actual union members had followed me home.

"All I can say is that this union is cultured to be like that. There's a hierarchy there, and the president and officers have spent years getting themselves elected to those posts. They have to be seen as people who get things done. Posturing is part of that."

"And the rest of them?" I wasn't happy with the number of eyes that were there simply to stare and intimidate at every meeting.

He chuckled, his mood lightening. "That's another story. Being part of the negotiation is considered a privilege. And intimidation is a key element of their strategy. It's just how it's always been done. The next person behind you is going to be treated the same way. And the next guy after that is going to get treated the same, too. Nothing you can do about it. You can't change the process. You just have to punch through. It's a system that's been around for over a hundred years."

I snorted. "So what you're telling me is that there are no shortcuts?"

He chuckled again. "That's funny."

I rolled my eyes.

He wasn't done trying to help. "Listen, every time they start getting nasty and selling you a bill of goods, stop listening. You've got to hear them in another way. Instead of whatever is coming out of their mouth, hear them asking for a paycheck to take home on Friday. If you can do that, that's all you need to hear. Everyone wants the same thing—it's just a matter of getting everyone to the point where they admit it."

So I headed back the next day and put myself in their shoes, just as he said to do. I studied and worked out the issues that were giving them the most heartburn. As I do with anyone, I tried to understand their motivations. What lay underneath their needs? I began listening in a better way—a way that allowed me to work within a system I wasn't going to be able to change.

Candy Store

Sometimes you have to give up in order to win.

I knew the local union leaders needed to show progress and build morale for the union members. I knew that any incentive or bridge building we did on the corporate side would give us opportunities to have fruitful negotiations.

They moved. We countered. We offered. They

declined. Back and forth it went. I gritted my teeth and kept myself from screaming, "But we all want the same things!" Nothing seemed to work. Everyone just wanted the easy win. And the easy win wasn't going to be good for anyone!

We were not making enough progress.

The idea of the candy store came to me after leaving a rather tough meeting. I was back in my office, and as I walked past my secretary's desk, I plucked a sweet from her open candy dish. I took a moment to unwrap and pop it into my mouth. I tasted the caramel and smiled.

And it hit me. I glanced back at the dish. If something small could break up the feeling after a bad day, what could we bring to the negotiations that would offer the same result? We were already breaking the larger issues into bite-size bits. What could we wrap up in gold foil and give to them, rather than making them fight for it?

We needed to compile a list of all the things that could be dealt with in a noncombative way, things that could create the positive atmosphere in the negotiations that we all so desperately needed. My team and I made a list of the things we, the management, cared about, and the things the union cared about. There were things we had taken for granted that we would give to the union, but we hadn't offered them yet. We made a list of these: Here were the candies we could offer.

Now we were prepared for any impasses. When progress seemed to hit a stalemate, we gave up some candy. These small offerings gave union leaders something to take back to their union members, something that allowed them to say, "This is what I have done for you," and this kept morale high. The result was just the momentum we needed to move us forward. We negotiated a good, solid, three-year contract, and we avoided a strike.

You Don't Have to Be the Smartest Person in the Room

No matter what level of management I was or how big my budgets were, there was always some element of the job that I did not understand. Always something that was foreign. Earlier in my career, I could study and learn quickly, but as my responsibilities grew, it was impossible to learn everything. My philosophy was to surround myself with people who were smarter than me.

Luckily, I had great employees and teams.

> Earlier in my career, I could study and learn quickly, but as my responsibilities grew, it was impossible to learn everything. My philosophy was to surround myself with people who were smarter than me.

In meetings, burgeoning technologies and the latest software initiatives were laid out for my purview. A proposed upgrade to our infrastructure could be a multibillion-dollar commitment, and I was responsible for the implementation—in other words, for recommending that the board of directors spend large amounts of money. My employees were the ones responsible for getting me to understand the details of each proposal. They brought an expertise that I knew to draw from. There was always something for me to learn.

In one particular case, I was preparing for a major presentation to request money from my boss for a large project. Every person that came into my office brought increasingly complex technical diagrams, until they began to blend together and look fuzzy. There was no way I could understand the issues, nor could I explain them to someone else in order to get approval for the budget we needed. I was drowning and needed a lifeboat. Fast. I needed a way to simplify this.

An image of ducks and bunnies popped into my head. The books I read to my sons at home when they were learning to read usually had farm animals (or dump trucks). My sons learned to grasp the meaning of the words by seeing the actions the ducks and bunnies were performing in the illustrations. "Duck went under a fence. See Duck? See the fence?" I would point out to them.

Sitting across from my team, I kept all this in mind. And evoking my duck and bunny image, I explained to them that we had to simplify and communicate without complex diagrams or we wouldn't get what we needed.

Thus, when dialogue didn't work, I used visual aids, starting with bar graphs and pie charts. When that didn't work, I simplified and tried again. When we came to an impasse, I learned to rephrase.

As with my boys, we never read a book just once. I was willing to go over the information again and again as needed.

Once I communicated my need for that simplification and review to my team, I appreciated what they were able to organize and simplify for me. As a result, I was able to fully grasp the situation, and I acquired the tools to make informed decisions.

Pride never should take the place of understanding.

Homeland Security—The Weight of the World

I tucked my briefcase into the space between my leg and the car door and looked out the window. The driver of the car I had just exited was pulling away in the opposite direction; the driver raised his hand in farewell. I waved back, then realized he probably couldn't see me due to this car's tinted glass. I dropped my hand back into my lap and turned to meet my new guide. Just as the tree-lined freeways in Virginia were different from the open highways in Denver, my Washington, DC–based team members were different, too.

My new driver regarded me in the same congenial but disciplined way I had been met with since arriving in our nation's capital. He smiled and lowered his sunglasses. "Welcome, ma'am." *The ma'am thing again.* "My name's Ray." He had short, dark hair that was tapered over his ears, military style. His shirt was starched with precise creases the humidity didn't even seem to touch. "I'm very happy that I'll be able to escort you today. How's your trip been so far?"

I reached up and lifted my hair off the back of my neck where it was sticking. "Busy. My trip's been busy." I knew my smile looked as wilted as my hair.

He nodded and reached over to change the settings

on the temperature controls. My side of the car came alive with a blast of cold air.

"How's that?"

It was like a siren's call. I turned my face toward the vent. "Better. Thanks."

Denver was hot, but this was something different. My shirt clung uncomfortably to my back every time I stepped outside. I didn't know if that was causing my overall state of nausea or if I was just getting sick. Either way, the heat wasn't helping.

Ray was all business, believing me settled. "Well, we're about thirty minutes away from the next meeting, give or take, depending on traffic." He picked up the manila envelope lying between us on the seat. "I have the security documents here that you'll need to sign beforehand. Same procedure. You're not to discuss anything we talk about today with anyone outside this program . . ."

I listened to him prattle through the same spiel I had heard now many times. *I know. I know.* It wasn't that I didn't appreciate the required protocol, but my stomach was beginning to roll and it made concentrating hard.

I took the forms he offered and signed them with his pen. It had taken nearly a year to arrive at this point. A year since I had moved from being the executive vice president and chief administrative officer to my current position as executive vice president of the business markets group, where I now managed, among other things, all of our government contracts. My security clearances were completed, I had been read in to the necessary programs (all referred to with letters and numbers), and I was finally in Washington to meet our US government customers. This was my third day in the city, and the previous two days had been a frenzied schedule of meetings held at officially undisclosed locations that conspiracy theorists argue may or may not exist. Because of the sensitive and necessarily compartmentalized nature of the federal work, I had to be taken to a nondescript location around the Metro DC area, where I would be handed off to the next program manager on my team so I could get securely to each briefing site. As I waited for each pickup, I felt like a live drop item waiting to be handed off to the next agent, as if I had somehow ended up in a classic spy movie.

I thought again how blissfully unaware I had been as a civilian, before taking this position, of the constant threat of danger I would face. Or how blissfully unaware I had been even of this trip. I was getting deluged with information,⁻ and now I was unnerved by how unacquainted I had been with the issues that came with global turmoil and world events. It was sobering for me to meet the government officials who were tasked with pondering the what-ifs of every conflict, disaster, or disturbance that pointed our way.

I felt plucked away from my corporate expertise and suddenly plunked down in the middle of a new setting without any personal experiences for reference. Other than a few college courses, I had never been an avid follower of foreign affairs. Rather than just focusing on Qwest's quarterly earnings and cash flow, these meetings were now getting me to envision war and the effects of cataclysmic events. How could I put into words my new concept of war and what it meant—and all that went with it? My hat is off to all the men and women who serve in our armed forces. But still, I didn't know if I was ever going to sleep easy again.

Ray and I made it to our meeting on time, and after yet another handoff and another briefing, by eight o'clock I was finally back in my hotel room, hunkering down for the night. I stared at the TV screen on mute in my room. Was I really this unnerved or was I getting the flu? I kept asking myself which one would be better.

I woke up the next morning, regretting that canceling my schedule was not an option. I now felt even worse than I had in the middle of the night, but I was going to have to pull myself together and push through.

Diana, my escort for the day, called my attention away from my queasiness. "It's just over there, between the trees. Can you see it?"

I did see it. It was peeking through a thick coverage of leaves, my final destination of the trip. I paused, taking the moment in. Was I headed to the White House for a briefing? I wanted to pinch myself. My awe was short-lived as another wave of nausea hit. "Okay, let's go," Diana said cheerily over my internal monologue. I pulled my purse strap up over my shoulder and tried not to stumble as we went forward.

The West Wing of the White House entrance finally loomed ahead, and I sighed with relief as the guard stepped up to greet us.

I took a second to glance around me as I left the screening area and walked down the hall toward our conference room. It was like walking into a movie set. I was in the hall with the black-and-white-checkered floor I had seen many times on television. It was long, and all the doors looked the same. I was escorted halfway down its length and into what was to be our meeting room.

In front of me, I was greeted by a sea of the usual testosterone. Uniforms, suits, and men—all the things I had come to expect in this type of setting. A few of the men looked pleasant, but the majority wore scowls.

We exchanged business cards, and as I looked at the official emblems on their cards, I noticed all of their cards had two titles. The first was always "Special Assistant to the President," and the second title was something like

"Homeland Security," "Cybersecurity Policy," "Cyberse-curity Coordinator," and "Resilience Policy," to name a few. I swallowed hard and thought I would be okay as soon as I could take my seat, but when I was seated, I realized I was wrong. I began to sweat as heavily as if the humidity had followed me inside. I had my hands clasped in my lap. I knew someone was speaking, but I couldn't hear anything over the rumble from my middle. The room wavered in front of me, the faces pitching into one another. I was going to be ill.

Behind my clouded vision, I knew what was about to happen and what it might look like if I didn't leave. It was becoming imperative that I move. My voice squeaked out as I stood. "Ah, I am so sorry, but can I step out for a minute to use the ladies' room?"

The face of the man seated next to me swam into focus and I saw him blanch. I wanted to tell him to be grateful I was being rude, but I also wanted to reassure him that I did know this was not the right thing to do, especially since everyone was there to talk with me. If he only knew the danger that everyone in the room was in, he would have encouraged my departure. I lurched to the door, and I heard someone belatedly mumble, "Ah, well, I guess."

Then I was in the hall, and the door shut out any other comments. I looked around and panicked. There was an endless sea of doorways and I had no idea which one led to the ladies' room. Breathing was becoming difficult. An intern walked around the corner. She was young and fresh looking, as if she couldn't have been happier doing what she was doing. I jumped in front of her and kept myself from reaching out to clutch her arm.

"Ladies' room?" I asked, trying to keep my voice steady.

She flew into action, and a shuffle or two later, I was vomiting alone in a bathroom stall.

I'm in the White House. This isn't right. I've got to get it together! But I wasn't in control anymore.

Diana's face tried to mask her concern as I slipped back into the room and took my place. She raised her eyebrows a little, and I answered her with a weak smile. She had run the meeting in my absence, and I let her manage the rest of it. I offered a comment or two, thanked the group, and was never so happy to get on a plane that evening. It was reported that the trip was considered a success. Other than Diana, no one realized how sick I had been. She had been all grins as she gave me a hug as her parting gift.

As I flew back to Denver, I took a moment to think about everything I had gone through. The White House was a little hazy in my memory, but I had done it. I represented our company, made decisions on the future, and participated in our homeland security, among other things. I was never so proud to be a United States citizen, and I was never so proud of each and every employee at Qwest for helping me be prepared.

I have to admit that when I got home I could not sleep for two weeks and had very bizarre dreams. I also gave my two sons extra-long hugs.

WORKPLACE ISSUES

As a leader, every little thing you do is noticed and matters. There was once a rumor that I had cancer because I looked tired and had lost weight. There was a rumor that I was going to eliminate a whole department because I did not smile at the VP of that department in the lobby. Once my boss even asked me if I was interviewing for a new job because I wore my best three suits for three days in a row. Leadership is a privilege, and we have to treat it accordingly.

Communications

Every morning when I logged onto my computer and checked my phone, I wished for fewer email and voice messages. But there wasn't a chance of that happening, so I waded in, grumbling, and tried to clear the cache as quickly as possible. For instance, I'd give myself fifteen minutes to read and respond to the first ten critical emails and for efficiency's sake, I kept my responses to one or two sentences.

Early on, I ignored the strange feedback I got from such email replies:

"Is something wrong?"

"I just got your reply; are you okay?"

"So, how are things going for you today? You seem a little tense."

Finally, a generous team member explained to me what was behind these responses.

"Your answers are just really, really short."

"Well, yeah, I'm answering their questions."

"But you don't answer the ones that aren't about work. You know, the questions about your day or about how you're doing."

"But I don't have time for small talk in email."

He sighed. "Okay, fair enough, but you also don't

even put the person's name at the top, or put in a *hi* or *hello* to start out with."

"But I've just hit *Reply*. It's going back to the person who sent it!"

He gave me a stern look. "You also don't close your email. At all. You just stop. At a period."

"What are you talking about?" I heard the defensiveness in my voice. "It's an office email!"

"Yeah, but you could put in 'have a nice day' or 'thank you' at the end," he offered.

In hindsight, this is still slightly funny to me. At home, I took the time to jot down a few words to help build and sustain my relationships with Pete, Jack, and Joe. But I didn't need to let anyone know it was me when I left a note saying "I love you!" So, why didn't that assumptive approach work in the office? *I answered your email, didn't I?* I wanted to ask. *Doesn't that show I care?*

Another day passed. I thought about it some more. Then I dismissed it. It was just too much for me to look at these office emails as something more than what I saw them as: a necessary evil rather than anything bordering on meaningful interaction. The idea was absurd! Email is for getting the job done, not for relationship building. I did not want to engage socially by writing those wretched emails. I couldn't justify the time it would take. So, I refused to change. My approach was firm. *Let's just get it done. We are professionals.*

I got away with that attitude—until I became COO. Then it mattered. There was a whole new group of people whom I could offend with a curt answer that might be misperceived.

With a heavy heart, I sat down at my computer and found myself stretching mentally for the right words. I warmed it up, waiting a sentence or two before I hit the nuts and bolts of the email. I included an opening and a closing, and I made sure to sign my name.

I had it in me the whole time. But that really wasn't the point!

The Fear of a First Day on the Job

Nothing is worse than feeling like you are the last person to find something out. Did I not hang out in the copy room enough? I should have gone to that last Friday night happy hour everyone else went to. All of those memories constantly reminded me that as a leader, I was going to do everything I could to communicate, communicate, communicate.

My first day after joining a large corporation with 75,000 employees was a lesson that I still often reflect upon. I use the following experience to remind myself to treat others as I would like to be treated, as well as the fact that even a quick note to let someone know what's going on can change the day.

After spinning through the circular sliding door in October 1988 on my first day at US West, I paused in the lobby, feeling dwarfed. I had entered into a beehive of activity, and my ears needed a second to adjust to the cacophony of conversations and movement that thrummed over and through the space.

Gathering my courage, I gripped my briefcase tighter and joined the stream that rushed toward the opening and closing jaws of the elevators. I reminded myself that I was lucky to have gotten the job.

I was the only person who exited on the sixteenth

floor. I checked my watch and smiled. I had arrived on my floor at five minutes to eight. Everything was going according to plan. *Timing the commute last week really paid off*, I said to myself.

A moment later the next elevator arrived, and I had to move out of the way of the flood of people getting off. They didn't even glance at me as they pushed past, but I followed them, hoping they would lead me to the floor's reception area.

I found an open seat and sat down. I had been instructed to wait there for someone to meet me.

No welcoming bandwagon arrived. Ten minutes later I was still waiting. I was annoyed that my punctuality was eroding. I bobbed a little in my chair, hoping that I could catch the receptionist's attention without being blatant. I couldn't.

Two minutes later I gave up. I stood up, ignoring the pinch of my shoes, and walked over to the desk. I cleared my throat.

The receptionist looked up from the form she was filling out.

I swallowed. "My name is Teresa Taylor. I was supposed to report to the sixteenth floor today for my first day of work."

The woman's eyebrows pulled together.

"Teresa Taylor?" she asked, as if it were a question. She turned over a few papers on her desk, as if there should be a piece of paper announcing my arrival, and then looked up at me, perplexed. "I don't have anything here that says anything about someone starting today." She leaned back in her seat and called out to a man whose head had just popped up from behind a partition wall. "You hear any-thing about a Teresa Taylor coming in today?"

He shook his head and disappeared again.

The woman turned back to me and shrugged.

I wanted to crawl under a desk. "Jerry Smith hired me. He said I was to report to the sixteenth floor," I repeated.

"Jerry Smith?" The furrow in her brows deepened. She shook her head.

I felt my face turning red. She really had no idea what I was talking about! Was this some elaborate hoax? Had I been interviewing for a real job? I threw out the last detail I knew about Jerry. "He's based in Des Moines?" My voice squeaked.

"Oh, Des Moines," she said, her eyes lighting up and her face softening. This meant something! She picked up her phone, ready to dial. "Now I gotcha. It'll be just a second, hon."

It took a little more than a second, but that was fine. I was too relieved to protest anything at that point.

"Okay, hon, just follow me." She stood up and I followed her around the back of her desk, down the aisle that passed between the cubicle-partitioned walls, until we reached what she announced was my new home.

I was being shown an open five-by-five-foot work area that contained four equally sized work spaces, three of which had a male colleague jammed into it. The fourth was waiting for me. Twenty-five square feet of coziness, like we had suddenly been thrown into a miniature pool together and told to swim.

She rattled off the names of the three men, who took turns shaking my hand. I blanched. I was going to have absolutely no privacy!

The receptionist left me with a cheery, "Welcome to US West," as I squeezed by the men to get to my chair.

For the first fifteen minutes, I chatted with my new "tubmates," and then the small talk petered out as they returned to their work.

In the next fifteen minutes, I found a home for the personal items I had brought with me in my briefcase.

In the fifteen minutes after that, I tried to ignore the press of humanity I felt at my back and stared instead at the bulky Macintosh computer that took up the majority of my workspace. I sat transfixed by it. It was like a stare down that I knew I was going to lose. I had never used a Mac before. I blinked. No one had said anything about using a Mac when I was hired. I would have remembered that.

And in the next fifteen minutes, I sat worrying about what to do next. I thought of trying to call Jerry, but the phone was being as helpful as the computer. My phone's lights flashed on and off like heart monitors attesting to life, but I didn't even know which was my line to use or how to dial out. I glanced at my watch. Only an hour!

How was I going to get through a day of this if I couldn't even make it through one hour?

A face popped around the corner just after nine. "Are you Teresa?" She was the first person who had spoken directly to me in over an hour. It was as though I had reached an oasis in a desert.

"Yes." I smiled up at her.

"I just got off the phone with Jerry. I know the four other members of your product team are based out of Seattle, but why don't you come join our meeting now to get your feet wet?"

I didn't cry. "I would love to." I grabbed a pencil and a pad of paper I had found tucked on a shelf and extricated myself from my cubicle without jostling everyone else.

Over the next few days, I came to learn that the reason no one was there to greet me was because rarely was anyone hired at my level from outside the company. With promotions happening internally, no one in my position would have expected to be pointed where to go and what to do. I was an anomaly, and I needed to catch up to the rest of my colleagues fast.

The woman who came to get me that first day eventually turned into a confidante and a lifetime friend. She not only showed me where I could look for help, but she often offered it before I knew to ask. She let me learn and showed me how to succeed.

With the right tools and focus, the fear I felt that first morning—the fear of possibly being in the wrong place or being out of my depth—quickly faded.

Leaders Keep Learning

My new job at US West was not entry level, but I was behind the curve since I had not grown up under the Bell system. So I signed up for each and every training class available for me to take. I took classes on the best ways to manage people, how to put together a successful team, and how to keep them motivated. Throughout the training sessions, I learned better ways to interview, to hire, *and* to fire. More important, I acquired the organization and prioritization skills that have served me ever since.

I went into each class with the idea that I would be the annoying one who always asked a crazy amount of questions. I figured this would be the best way for me to get a leg up.

Although the eagerness of those first few years eventually wore off, attending training sessions had become a habit for me. So I went on to tackle issues like financial analysis. I attended diversity training, community-giving seminars, and anything related to our company's marketing.

Not every course I went to was new or earth-shattering, but I never regretted taking part in the training that I did. It kept my skill set sharp and gave me a chance to sit back and evaluate some of the things I took for granted. Intuition only takes you so far, and it can always be fine-tuned with training and experience. These classes provided both.

As my roles grew in the company, I was offered enrollment at many seminars, workshops, and clinics outside of the company. I took every one I could. A few times I was sent off to a weeklong "school" to have one of my flaws corrected. It was part of my "personal development"—code for "you have a weakness that better get fixed soon!"

Even though I was always irritated by this type of coaching, I learned to make the best of it. When I look back now, I can see that those were valuable times, and I still page through the assessments or books once in a while to review them.

> Take advantage of any learning you're offered. Act like a sponge and take in as much as you can. You are never done learning.

Take advantage of any learning you're offered. Act like a sponge and take in as much as you can. You are never done learning.

Teamwork

In general, whenever I obtained a new role, it was because something was not working well in that department and my job was to fix it. In any new role, I pulled individuals from around the company for my team. I was desperate to have new strategies, and I needed a group that could quickly learn and find resolutions.

> The key element in putting together a high-performance team is to value each individual as a whole person.

The key element in putting together a high-performance team is to value each individual as a whole person. It is not just about the job at hand; it is caring about who the person is inside and outside the workplace. I needed individuals who could care about each other. And in turn, they would be able to care about the rest of the employees.

My teams needed to be exceptional. It started with my attitude toward the selection process. I wasn't looking to strong-arm anyone, nor was I looking to drive anyone into the ground. I hoped that all the men and women on my team had a family to go home to at the end of the day.

Stronger and better teams are not led by widow-makers.

Who you put in what job is the key. The HR department gave me many tips on how to interview, what questions to ask, and on how to let the interviewee do all the talking. I learned to master the open-ended questions:

Tell me your three strengths.

Can you share with me your three weaknesses?

Can you give me a scenario where you . . .

Is there anything specific you would like to share with me?

But these weren't enough.

I found that the best interviews took place outside the office and involved a meal. Breakfast, lunch, or dinner would do. You can make so many observations when watching someone order a meal and eat. For example, how do they treat the server? Do they acknowledge that person? (I'm always sensitive to this, since I made a living as a waitress during college.) Do they say "thank you" when something is brought to them, or are they rude?

How they order the meal is crucial. Can they even make a decision? For goodness sake, if they can't order lunch, how are they going to run a department for me? I would immediately cringe when the individual wanted to order "off-menu" or make three "substitutions." That was a blinking neon sign to tell me that this person I might end up managing was going to be in the "high maintenance" category. Of course, an overabundance of alcohol consumption at dinner was a deal killer. Several times I was close to offering a person a job and changed my mind after having a meal with them. When I did not go with my instincts on this, I always regretted my hiring decision and had to deal with the consequences later.

One of the roles in leading a team is to keep everyone motivated.

I had employees who had grievances. Sometimes it was about a micromanaging supervisor or a difficult work environment; at other times, it was about the particular employee's personal issues that were spilling over into the workplace. But whatever their grievances might have been, I asked the same questions.

"Are you getting new experiences? Do you feel like you're growing, that you are changing, learning?"

If they said yes, then we would talk about what issues were holding them back. If they said no—and if they had been threatening to leave the company or had told me about another job offer—I'd simply tell them, "If you are unhappy here, and you're not learning anything, and someone has offered you another opportunity that looks good, take it."

No ploy. No agenda. I wasn't firing them! I just knew that for me, personally, I wasn't happy unless there was a challenge to tackle or a cause to champion. Why wouldn't I assume this employee sitting across from me would feel the same way?

Over the years, I received a number of phone calls—in some cases a few weeks later, in others after a few months—from former employees who thanked me for the advice to leave. An intangible value to growing as a person is through challenges, and I was never going to hold someone back from achieving their goals, because I myself lived for success.

The privileges of leadership come with the intangibles of leadership. You can't go to a class or get a degree in leadership. You have to live and breathe it. You have to always ask yourself: "How would I feel if someone talked to me that way or made this decision without asking my opinion?" People want to be heard. I once told my boss that I would be loyal to his decisions, even if I disagreed, but that I wanted five minutes to share my point of view. Once I had said my piece, I could get over it if the decisions went a different direction. As with parenting, it is crucial to have unity at the top.

The most difficult transition in a career is the day when you realize *you can't do* the work anymore, and now you have to *do it through others*. You don't have to be the smartest person in the room, but you do have to be smart when choosing your team. A team is like a puzzle, and each part needs to fit together. When the piece doesn't fit anymore, look for another one.

PART IV

BETWEEN THE LINES—
INTEGRITY & ETHICS

Some executives gave me the feeling they couldn't care less. They had the title and the power, but they didn't have the humanity. I, on the other hand, was losing sleep. Lots of sleep. I never had a problem falling asleep, but I never stayed asleep for very long. I would roll out of bed to make lists and notes to myself. And when I would finally catch a few winks, I would always dream about work. I would talk in my sleep about work. I would "hold meetings" and "negotiate deals" as I flopped around restlessly next to Pete. My worst nights were the ones when I had to deal with downsizing. I had endless dreams about what it was going to mean to this person or to that group. I especially hated laying off people who did their jobs well but who had to be let go for budgetary reasons.

The novelty of my stress fed into Pete's wicked side. He began to appreciate my nighttime ranting because it gave him something to talk about when my team or colleagues would get together socially. He would call out in jest to a team member passing by, "Hey, Kevin, just so you know, she fired you in her sleep last night!" Or he would sidle up to someone I was working closely with and whisper sympathetically: "Monica, I hate to break it to you, but last night Teresa tossed out your latest budget proposal!"

In the hope of thwarting Pete's fun and improving the quality of my sleep, I read everything I could about how to sleep better. And I tried nearly every technique I read about. I visualized beaches and other vacation spots. I breathed deeply and practiced mindfulness. During the union negotiations, at the end of a two-day, forty-eight-hour nonstop session, I had a short reprieve in which to sleep before having to head back to the bargaining table. My boss knew I struggled with getting rest, so he suggested I try a shot of tequila (or two), even if it was ten in the morning, in order to sleep throughout the six hours open to me. I thought, why not? I was just desperate enough to try.

Because my family was out of town that weekend, Suzanne, a friend of mine, came to my house to check on me later that day. She didn't know what to do when she saw me lying fully clothed, snoring and slobbering all over the bedspread, at three in the afternoon.

I was even willing to follow bad advice in order to stop the chatter going on in my head. Short of caring less and becoming more callous, there wasn't any other viable solution.

I've been asked why I kept working if I was affected in that way and felt everything so keenly. That, happily, had an easy answer: because I loved my job.

The concern keeping me up at night was the same one that kept me coming in every day: the challenge of blowing past the expectations of shareholders and board members, plus the excitement of staying competitive through innovation. It was everything I looked for.

MODELING BEHAVIOR

I wanted to make a difference, and I was determined to find a way to do just that. I had some idea of what it meant to care about people and the company before working with Dick Notebaert, one of the CEOs I've had the privilege of working under. But he really drove the concept home for me. I had an inkling of it, but he was a huge mentor in that capacity.

He expected me to be a leader by modeling the behavior I expected from my team members. I knew the message was that it was all about how those ideas were articulated and modeled. "If you are ever not sure about something," he said, "ask yourself what your mom would say if it was on the front page of the newspaper. How would you feel about it? You can't act differently in a restaurant at night than you act at work. You are always on."

He and I believe that when you are at the top, people watch you, and you need to set the example and model desirable behavior. He put it simply: "You come in early so people see you come in early. You leave late so they see you leave late." Even what I was wearing was open for discussion. He crystallized for me that everything I did on the job was a reflection of me and my ethics. The moment when you have to make a decision about something— "Should we sign this deal? Should this be covered? Should we spend the company's money on something?"—or the moment when you sign contracts with a customer: These are the moments when it's vital to live ethically.

Whenever I asked an employee to do something, I asked myself: "Am I doing this as well?" The idea was to walk in their shoes and decide if you could be comfortable walking where they were being asked to walk. It wasn't about leading. It was based on the idea of caring enough that others would follow, about winning the respect of those doing the work. I still needed to take action that was difficult, but I never believed that I existed in a vacuum.

Why did I follow Dick's advice? Because I saw the results. By following his approach, he got everyone on the same page. I saw that when everyone in the company understood the values he represented, saw how he intended the customers to be treated, and knew the direction we were going and what we were trying to accomplish, then all oars were rowing the same way. And, wow, did I see the results.

This is my definition of leadership.

It wasn't about leading. It was about caring enough that others would follow.

Compromise—The Danger of Being Untrue to Yourself

I glanced up at the TV and felt a familiar wrench in the gut. It is a feeling that doesn't fade. Over a year had passed since I left what was once Qwest and had now become CenturyLink, and seeing a story about additional layoffs taking place there still gave me pause.

It was the worst part of my job.

Like many industries before mine, the end of the traditional phone service—that piece of Americana known as *the Phone Company*—was fading. At board and employee meetings alike, I was always announcing constricting forecasts in the telecommunications market. I felt like a predictor of the apocalypse.

I'd driven past enough telephone poles dwarfed by cell towers to wonder how much longer those wires would still be humming. I had only to look at the miles and miles of abandoned railroad tracks lying empty beneath 747s on their approaches to airport runways to know what the future held for us. I was an instrument of change in the industry, and it was painful for both of us.

Our company's shrinking bottom line affected employment, stocks, and pensions, and it ultimately led to our merger with CenturyLink. The merger made layoffs inevitable.

The battles that led up to that merger were fierce for

many years. In order to allow the company to recover from less profitable divisions, we needed to cut the workforce in one area so that we could compensate by creating new areas. All the while, I needed to keep our employees focused on our customers rather than on internal issues, which was the only way to make sure that we had customers to provide for. As my positions became more elevated, the responsibilities became greater.

I remember one Saturday morning when my son and I entered the local Apple store to browse. He stood over the new iPad, and we were both captivated by the graphics and color. My son swiped his fingers across the screen and looked up at me expectantly.

"No, no. I said we were just looking today!"

"But Mom, look!" He pushed the iPad at me again and I pushed it back.

"When did it suddenly become okay to push a seven-hundred-dollar piece of tech at me and think that I'm just going to buy it?"

Joe smiled. "But it's not for me, it's for Dad."

I laughed and walked toward the iPhones, which was the original errand that had brought us into the store.

It was then that I felt eyes on me from one of the customers hunched over a computer. He was seated on a stool and had not looked at the screen for over thirty seconds. Something about the way he was focusing on us made my skin crawl. Qwest had just entered another round of layoffs, and with the story covered in the news and plenty of people who knew who I was, I wondered if this was a former employee, or someone's husband or friend, who felt that the Apple store was as good a place as any to air his grievances. I turned halfway around and pushed Joe so that he was in front of me and angled away from the man.

A salesperson walked up to us, and I explained we wanted to take a look at the new iPhone. He smiled and said he was happy to help us. When I turned around, the man at the computer was no longer there. Instead, he was standing next to me.

He asked me if I was Teresa Taylor.

I took a big gulp, paused, and said, "Yes, I am."

My heart was racing and I wasn't sure what to expect next. It would not be the first time that someone decided they wanted to tell me in person how mad they were that I had laid them or one of their family members off.

"I saw you speak at one of our employee meetings, and I just wanted to meet you in person," the man said.

We small-talked for a minute about the department he worked in, and he moved on.

I sighed.

That was not the only time I was noticed in public, but not every encounter I had was positive. I had learned to be cautious.

When I spoke to employees about layoffs, I never held back how I felt. But my regret wasn't going to pay the mortgages or put food on the table for those who now needed to find other ways to support their families. And I couldn't point to the jobs I was saving and say, "But these people will still have a job!" This didn't change the reality for that particular employee.

I mentioned before that I didn't sleep well for many years because of worrying about how my decisions would impact the workforce I led. I wish it could have been different, but I'm glad that my anxiety never faded. As Dick Notebaert taught me: "The day you go home and you're not upset that you laid people off is the day you are in trouble." He'd lean over the desk and say: "If you go home and say woo, no big deal, then I'm worried about you!"

He'll never have to worry.

Since I hated being fearful, I chose to live both my professional and my personal life in such a way that I would not give myself unnecessary reasons to fear. I always erred on doing what was right versus what would have made me popular.

Be forewarned that this decision is not always pleasant or easy.

Front Page Headlines

At Qwest, my office would move with each new assignment and promotion. The elevator was the still point in my turning world as I changed floors and responsibilities. But no matter the change, one thing that remained constant was my assigned parking spot—once I finally had one.

Self-governance is like that parking space. It's fixed and permanent, even when situations or positions change. Self-governance is rule based and immovable, and it creates the faith in yourself that as long as you play by the rules, the system you've invested in will, in the end, swing any imbalance back to the right side of things.

> As long as you play by the rules, the system you've invested in will, in the end, swing any imbalance back to the right side of things. It is this belief that is key to an individual employee and a corporation being truly successful.

It is this belief, coupled with good self-governance, that is key to an individual employee and a corporation being truly successful.

So, I lived by rules that I wouldn't break.

When there was an imbalance, I would wait patiently or impatiently—it didn't matter—for the day of reckoning that would always come. A pendulum is always in motion.

The hardest wait was when US West was purchased by Qwest. For a brief period of time, Qwest was led by a CEO who made headlines for his unique personality. Within days of his assuming control of the company, I learned that nothing was going to be considered off-limits. Not our workplace code of conduct. Not employee life issues. Not our obligations outside the workplace to our families and friends.

This CEO would often announce last-minute meetings that seemed terminal in length. We would hunker down at his command around the conference table, even on the evening of Valentine's Day, before, during, and long after any and all dinner reservations had been missed. Many had to slip in a phone call with a hasty apology to their significant other. The CEO's attitude was shaped by the fact that his own spouse stayed on the other side of the country, so what was it to him to make every other employee work with the same detachment? If the spouses or partners were angry, how was it *his* problem? *He* had found *his* solution.

Even with all the personal sacrifices and the longer hours, there was a feeling of hopelessness that our efforts were not bearing any fruit. If anything, what the company was harvesting was increasingly bad.

If hours were spent haggling out a solution to a particular problem and if a solution had finally been reached, it would be decreed moot and thrown out on a dime, rendering all the previous work pointless.

Stress built, and the old days of camaraderie were obliterated. His leadership style permeated the whole company. With the increased tension, we all had to be careful where we stepped. Dissension among the rank and file was encouraged and cultivated. We were to compete against each other at every turn: the louder our arguments, the better. To be on top, you were told to fight, to wound whomever you wished, to take it.

It was as if the teeming streets of ancient Rome had taken over the active hallways at Qwest, and the competition for survival—like scenes played out in the Colosseum—had taken over our conference room.

Caesar filled the head of the table with his presence. We were the audience for his games. The chosen gladiators of the day held dry erase markers and laser pointers instead of swords and shields, but we were expected to cause similar wounds. A few staff members embraced the new approach for consensus seeking. They seemed to feel the sting less, and their eyes shone with the coming battle. The rest of us were the beleaguered prisoners brought up from the cells below. We were being allowed to witness the coming scene so that we could fully appreciate what was to come.

After the battle ended, we would wait to see who was to be declared the champion. Would the figurative thumb point up or down?

As in Rome, the frenzy never ended with this seeming power struggle over life and death. Power crept and crawled with its cousin Greed into corners that may or may not have known their influence before. Latent desires and perceived wrongs seemed to twist and turn in the winds of justification.

It was exhausting. I limped away from each meeting just glad to be drawing breath, and I drove home like a maniac. The air was clean outside, and I became surer the closer to home and my family I got. I would never have survived the bruising and punishing assaults without them.

I held onto the fact that all things run their course.

Even Rome fell.

In 2002, the Securities and Exchange Commission and the Department of Justice arrived on Qwest's doorstep, and the questioning of what had taken place during the CEO's tenure began to play out.

I went to my first interview with the investigators and sat down, fighting the urge to kick my shoes off underneath the table. The lawyers who questioned me held no fangs for me. I sighed as the questions began. I had nothing to hide. I had done nothing to be ashamed of. I had endured the ridicule and the loss of favor by standing my ground, even when it had seemed hopeless, even when all my faith in righting the system felt as if it had been reduced to something the size of a mustard seed. I clung on.

My answers to the investigators and lawyers were easy.

"No, I did not."

"No, never."

"No."

Indictments and firings swept through the building as fast as once-great ancient cities had been reduced to embers. I watched the burning, the firing, the wailings. Thankfully, I never had anything to worry about. I had no reason to fear scrutiny because I had lived my professional life without compromises.

Maturity/Judgment Calls

The greatest failures I've seen in my corporate life were due to the selfishness and greed of others. They brought down more than one corporate head.

Yet I never understood the attraction to selfishness and outrageous greed by which some colleagues and associates lived personally and professionally. I knew many who were doomed because of their lack of integrity. They weren't grounded. They didn't have a rudder.

I knew I was different. The typical executive who gets to the level that I had gotten to had been married multiple times, had numerous kids, and talked about every single member of his or her family in a negative way. I've heard children be called leeches, wives be called worse. None of these executives were open to the fact that they were also parents who were responsible for participating in raising their kids, or to the fact that their marriages could fail from lack of care just as often as businesses did.

I didn't get pulled into the cycle of greed; it was a simple choice for me. I just didn't deviate from what I knew was ethical and right. I had a rudder. I might have winged it a lot along the way, even gone with the flow, but in the end, I knew there were things I just wasn't willing to do, no matter how attractively someone tried to paint them for me. This did not make for a pleasant environment at work, but I knew that whatever was dumped on me there, at least I could go home and everything would be okay. There were days when I drove home really fast, happy to get away, happy to see my husband and my boys.

I remember being summoned into the conference room on the fifty-second floor of our building, where this particular CEO was waiting with his direct report team. They wanted me to explain to him why we could not do what they had requested we do with a specific product offering. I had already been asked this same question and had given the same answer, but my boss and his peers did not like my answer—or at least when they had relayed it to the CEO, he hadn't liked the answer.

When I entered that conference room, I knew this was the day that I could be fired. I wasn't going to change my position. I really didn't care; I almost hoped it would happen so that I would be put out of my misery.

Several times I tried to answer the questions the CEO was asking me, but each time, someone in the room interrupted me and I could not answer.

I finally blurted out, "Joe, could I talk to you alone?"

I have no idea what possessed me to say that, and I

couldn't even believe I had. Nobody moved, and there was a very long silence. I could feel everyone glaring at me, but I just kept my eyes forward. My heart was pounding hard, and I broke into a sweat.

Joe said, "Yes, that's a good idea."

Yet nobody moved, and again there was a long silence. Now I did not know what to do, so I just sat there and did not budge.

Joe yelled, "What is wrong with all of you! @#$! Get out of here. I just said I wanted to talk to her alone." (I don't think he even knew my name.)

Slowly, each person got up and left the room. Every one of them gave me a look as they passed me. I could feel their eyes burning into my skin. One person stayed because he always did.

"You too, Drake."

After Drake left, I explained to the CEO why we could not do what was being suggested. I talked slowly and was very calm. After a brief, productive, even-keeled conversation, Joe said, "You are right. Thank you for explaining this to me."

That was it, that simple.

I thanked him for his time and left the conference room. Then I took the elevator down to my office and waited for my boss to call and fire me. Nothing happened. The phone didn't ring; he didn't stop by my office. Absolutely nothing. *How could this be?*

That day I was willing to lose my job over my decisions. I did not have another job or a lead on a new job. I was the main source of income in our family, and I had two little boys. As I sat in my office staring out the window, I asked myself: *What were you thinking?*

While I did not get fired, I did get presented with another consequence. Shortly thereafter, my boss told me that I had to move my office to the fifty-second floor. This was unheard of and not what I wanted. Now I was at the CEO's beck and call, but at least I felt good about myself—and I still received a paycheck every other Friday.

Rudders

As you continue to mature, your rudders become more and more clear.

You continue to know more and more about where your motivation is coming from and what is directing your actions.

Again and again I was motivated by the three men in my life. Even if they were in trouble or rude, even if they took me for granted and sent me crying to my room because they forgot something important to me, I still knew my direction, and I was grounded because of those two growing boys and their father who populated my life. Since I had identified my rudder early, this meant that I still made it home at night, even as my income and responsibilities grew. I didn't go sideways. I also didn't get full of myself, because in the opinion of the people who mattered most, the greatest thing I had done was to have married the one and have given birth to the two others. Factor in that when our sons bragged about their parents at school, they usually bragged about Pete. It may be cool that a helicopter had picked their mom up from the house before, but it was their dad who had put out a forest fire.

The Cost of Being Right All the Time

A reality that every married couple goes through is that you don't always get along.

When those arguments would come up between Pete and me, a week might go by, at the end of which I would have to ask myself: *Did I say anything loving all week, or was I just bitchy?* Even if we had been angry with one another for a week, though, we still kept our set-in-stone, will-happen, priority date nights. No matter what, we'd get a babysitter because we knew that dating was connecting, and that any connection was better than nothing at all, especially during the hard times.

We'd go to see a movie, and questions like "Is this seat okay?" felt like code for "I'm not apologizing for this one!" If our arms bumped on the armrest as we sat down, there was a moment of decision over who would be the one to retreat. But then a moment later, one of us would have second thoughts. It might have been as uncomfortable as the Cold War at times, but just as with the Cold War, eventually a period of détente would defrost our icy attitudes, and a consolatory bucket of popcorn would be offered.

The rest of the night we'd spend feeling each other out, but by the end, when we'd ask, "How did you like the movie?" we might also mean: "Give me some more time to get over this." More than likely, though, it was our way of saying, "I'm really over this."

A response of, "The movie was good" would then be code for, "Funny, because I'm over it, too!"

Even if it felt as if we were warily circling each other and inching closer throughout the whole night, we would know—without screaming or the need to throw anything—where we were and what we needed to work on in order to get to a better place.

The attempt to connect brought more to the table than the most perfect date night ever did. It was through those difficult times that we learned the value of pushing through when it was hard. But those moments were only possible when we were honest about our role in the argument and when we could admit where we had been wrong.

It is okay to be wrong and admit it sometimes.

Difficult relationships at work can be as painful to maneuver through, but the same fortitude that makes a successful marriage also applies to platonic and professional relationships. All quality relationships require communication. All of them will at times feel like one partner is just going through the motions of getting along with the other, but a bad situation will naturally right itself—especially if you don't have to be right all the time.

> All quality relationships will at times feel like one partner is just going through the motions of getting along with the other, but a bad situation will naturally right itself—especially if you don't have to be right all the time.

Teaching Children to Make Good Choices

Raising children is probably the single largest test of your own integrity and ethics. They are stimulated by so many things, from TV, social media, and friends, to teachers, coaches, and cousins. Each one of these interactions is a choice and a consequence. How do you teach your children to make good choices?

When our children were young, we innocently introduced them to the Tooth Fairy, Easter Bunny, and Santa Claus. We were excited to create this pretend fantasy world for them. In many ways, Pete and I relived our childhood through them.

Being the Tooth Fairy was probably our most challenging role because it seemed that between the two boys, there was always a tooth that fell out and that needed to be wrapped and put under either Joe's or Jack's pillow. It was then up to Pete or me to remember to sneak into the boys' bedroom after they fell asleep, reach under the appropriate pillow, find the tooth in the dark, and replace it with a few coins. If we forgot, the sad face in the morning was devastating. When that happened, we said that the Tooth Fairy must have had a hard time getting to our house because there was stormy weather. Luckily, they never really knew whether it had stormed during the night, so they believed us.

This routine was exhausting, and Pete and I would ask each other: "How many more teeth do they have?"

One night Pete was in charge of being the Tooth Fairy and thought he had successfully accomplished the task. In the morning, however, Joe announced that he had been awake when Pete exchanged the tooth for coins. He matter-of-factly stated: "There is no Tooth Fairy," and the look on his face was so sad.

Then it got worse. "That must mean there's not an Easter Bunny?" he continued, tears forming. And then he asked the big one: "There's no Santa Claus?" Now it was full out crying. He was very upset, and our instinct as parents was to keep the game up so that he would stop crying and be the happy little boy that he was. As a parent, you feel absolutely awful. It is more than the crying. Your child looks at you as if he or she is saying: "You lied to me; you're horrible; you've ruined my life . . ."

But we did tell him the truth and tried to console him. Pete, in particular, spent extra time spoiling him. The emotions and consoling went on for weeks. Eventually time passed. We still reflect on it, and now Joe will laugh with us when we retell the story. I am not really sure what he is going to do when he has children.

These moments continue as your children mature. With each new year came more times where we were faced with deciding how truthful to be. Where is the line between telling them the full truth or twisting it slightly because they aren't mature enough for the full truth?

The questions just kept coming: "Did you and Dad smoke pot?"; "Did you drink when you were in high school?"; "Did you ever lie to your parents?"; "Did you have a party at your house when your parents were gone?"; "Did you ever cheat on a test?"; "How much money do you make?"

Pete and I did not pretend that we were perfect as children. If we told them something bad we did when we were young, we also shared the consequences with them. In particular, I believe the teen years are when children are the most vulnerable. You can't be with them all the time, so you hope that when they are faced with decisions, they will make good choices. For a long time, I told them that I had a way of knowing everything they did, and they actually believed me for a few years. I absolutely used the threat to keep them on their toes.

The best you can do is keep talking to them, even when they don't want to talk. Take the few moments they give you and come up with excuses to have them spend time with you. (For boys, food is always a good option.)

Sometimes they don't want to be with you and they make that clear, but we pushed the issue anyway.

Teaching your children ethics and integrity at a young age is the best lesson you can give them. You have to give them the rudders and model the behavior. They are always watching and observing how you respond and react. Be careful how you speak, even comments you might make when watching the news, sharing about your day at work, or talking about a friend.

The best gift you can give them is strong ethics.

Time flies. I knew my children would grow up. I knew they would leave—that they *should* leave—but the reality of it didn't crystallize for me until I had to enter Jack's room to sort his things in preparation for his departure to college. Suddenly my drop-in visits to his room had an expiration date. The thought nearly crushed me. I felt tears welling up in my eyes, and there was no place for me to go with them, so I hurriedly reached for a box and began to tape it, trying to ignore the tears dripping down my face. I just couldn't believe that this moment had arrived. It was real. It was tangible. I had carried this kid around in me for nine months, raised him for eighteen years, and now I felt like he was just being ripped away! I glanced over at him pulling shoes from the bottom of his closet. I fought valiantly against the urge to grab onto him and say, "Hey, wait, don't go. Don't go."

I turned away and wiped my tears with the back of my hand as I spun the tape around to ready it for the next box. But Jack had seen.

"Oh, Mom . . ." He came around the end of the bed to give me a hug, which made me cry even more!

I cried regularly up to the moment of his leaving. The day before, Pete sat me down. He had been watching me mope around the house. My shoulders were sagging as I made laps, trying to see if I had overlooked something. Had Jack left a book or jacket out that he would need to take with him the next day? As I came into the living room to check one more time, Pete stood up and held me gently but firmly by the shoulder. He stood across from me and his face turned serious—all the lines drawn in, probably the same look he used when hazing a mountain lion at work.

"Now listen, Teresa. Tomorrow, don't let Jack's last sight of you be you crying the whole time we are moving him into his dorm. That'll just make him feel bad."

I melted instantly. He was right. I had no desire to be a cliché. It was one thing to cry at home, but this was different. This was going to be our official good-bye, and I could picture what a disaster it could turn out to be. Me sobbing, waving until that bend in the road would rob me of the last sight of my son. I shuddered and nodded. I was glad that Pete had gotten in front of the mountain lion.

"Good." He sighed again and went into the kitchen. I glared after him. Secretly, I thought he was being more than a little indifferent about the whole thing. He seemed like he wasn't even upset. It was then that I noticed there was a little more heaviness in the way *his* feet were moving. I felt myself smile. *Softie.*

The day arrived. We had packed up Jack's truck the night before, and we were caravanning with his new roommate and his parents. I kept my mind busy as we drove. I tried not to think about how I was taking my son to his new school, to his dorm, carrying in our car the things he would move into his new room. When we got there, I tried not to be so conscious of the click of my flip-flop as I entered the room that was to be his new home for the coming year. I swallowed hard more than once.

And all I can say is, I tried. I really tried. I really, really tried. Hard. And I did it!

I had clamped my jaw tight. Grinned until my cheeks

hurt and blinked to keep my vision clear. It was through sheer willpower that I managed to give a small cheery wave as we pulled away at the end of the day. I turned around in my seat and faced forward and just managed to wait long enough to get one mile down the road before the faucet turned on. We were now in the car, all four of the parents. Sue and I had begun to sob. I had company. I handed her a Kleenex. We blew in unison.

Once we arrived back home, everything felt off. The whole tone of the house seemed to change with Jack's departure. His truck wasn't parked in its spot in the driveway. His room was empty and clean. (That was *not* normal.) None of his friends were knocking at the door. Where we sat at the dinner table felt weird.

Poor Joe. He was bound to pay the price of Jack's departure. Over the next few weeks, he glanced up at me more than once at the dinner table to find me staring at him. I would try to cover by quickly offering him more to eat. When I came in to check on how he was doing on his homework, I would linger in the doorway. He would watch me from the corner of his eye. If I stood there too long, he would look up.

"What?"

I'd try not to look like I was scurrying away.

I just mothered him to death.

And I felt justified.

As I reflected on how fast the eighteen years went by, my biggest concern was that I hadn't taught Jack everything he needed to know before leaving home. But, of course, that isn't possible. All of a sudden I was thinking of moments I should have handled differently. Maybe I was too hard on him; maybe I should have been home more; maybe I didn't spend enough time with him.

Jack's leaving for college was one of the times when I questioned my motherhood. When I watched him during his brief visits home over the next few months, however, I knew I had done the best I could and that he was evolving into a very confident, strong young man. I was proud: He was going to be just fine!

PART V

CONNECTIONS

Networking is about working through a loose grouping of individuals to create openings and opportunities that can help you leverage yourself into a more solid and viable position. That is the power of networking—or rather, connecting. I prefer the word *connecting* because it feels more sincere than *networking*. Maybe that's because I came from the telecommunications industry, where networking referred to computers, fiber optics, servers, and such.

Van, my hairdresser, is a master at connecting. He has a unique place in many women's lives. I laugh because there is no one else that I've spent such focused yet chatty time with for an hour or two, every six weeks, for fifteen years. Much like a priest, he has become privy to the ongoing details of my life—my family, career, and relationships, the whole deal. And although I feel special, he has the same relationship with each and every one of his clients. For many years, he knew where I worked, but he had no idea about the level of my titles, and it didn't matter.

So, why is he my idol when it comes to networking? Because he truly listens and remembers what we talked about six weeks ago. He cares and is sincere. One particular month I repeatedly had to cancel and reschedule my appointment because I was buried at work. He called me and asked if it would be helpful if he opened the shop early and met me at 6:00 a.m. so that I could get my hair cut and colored. My guess is that he had done that many times before for other clients.

In return, I offer him loyalty, referrals, and respect. I always make sure I am on time because I don't want to ruin his schedule. Many of my friends see Van, and each of them is treated just as I am. He also connects us and fills each of us in on what the other is doing—not in a gossipy way, but through a sincere conversation that often benefits both parties.

BUILD CIRCLES—
PERSONAL RELATIONSHIPS

Although my best friend, Robin, might affectionately see me solely as an ultra-professional networker—one who perhaps overattends corporate events—I see connecting as something that goes far beyond its business connotations. I see it as something that every parent, friend, couple, or single does in her or his everyday life.

We establish relationships with those around us, be they neighbors or coworkers.

We strengthen bonds, be it with families or friends.

We build these relationships because of a common need we have. When we initially meet someone, we start talking to that person and find commonality between us. Later, we might make a more formal use of those connections, but in the beginning, we are simply looking for camaraderie, with no real agenda at all.

I believe that when done right, these relationships benefit everyone involved. The process of connecting is about building rather than simply about working.

> The process of connecting is about building rather than simply about working.

Befriend the Parents of Your Child's Classmates

As a working mom, I had to deal with the issue of making sure that my sons could get back and forth to all their extracurricular activities. Soccer practice was particularly challenging because it was so early in the evening. On the first day of practice, when all the kids began their drills and broke in their brand new shoes, I wandered up to the parents milling in groups. I would take note of the ones who seemed to have just come from work. I struck up conversations with other mothers who looked like me. I didn't have to meet every single parent. Which ones had kids my son interacted with? I wanted to meet them.

When a connection was made, we all immediately pulled out our BlackBerrys and entered our contact information. Later I'd be able to call and ask: "Do you mind bringing Jack home from practice today?" And the next time, I would get a call from a mom asking me if I could give her son a ride because she was going to be late.

You first meet other parents, teachers, and coaches because you want to know who your children are spending time with and what they are doing. But it's also about creating a network that anyone can use to seek help and support. That network can also provide job leads, customer referrals, tips on finding a good tutor, guidance on what teacher to request for third grade, and so on.

This interaction is a source for connecting, interrelating, and building relationships.

At one point, I wanted to set up day care services between my children's elementary school and our local YMCA. I couldn't transport my children to after-school day care during work hours, and I knew other parents were dealing with the same challenge. It was the previous connections and networks I had built up with those other parents that provided the leverage we needed in order to create an after-school day care at our children's elementary school. Once I had the initial meetings with the school administration and the local YMCA, these networks made it easy to gather the other mothers, and then we were a force to be reckoned with. My involvement was the natural by-product of being engaged, paying attention, and listening to the other parents I was coming into contact with at the school.

What Is a Friend?

In this age of social media, the more connections you have on LinkedIn, the more important you are—or so the concept goes. If you have 500+ connections, people think you are really networked.

I jokingly say that I really have only one girlfriend—Robin. That is because I truly can call her at any time of the day or evening and she will answer. I also have a small number of women friends, however, and each one is extremely important to me, as they provide a perspective and warmth you cannot get from men. Sisters-in-law are also a gift that I did not expect from marriage, and I am very fortunate that Tonya and Terry entered my life through Pete's brothers. You can really let your hair down over a glass of wine with your sisters-in-law, and nothing is off limits during a conversation.

But it takes a lot of energy to have true friends, and for a long time, my marriage was the sole relationship that I had the capacity to focus on. Friends also come and go as changes in your life happen. When I was first out of college, my roommates were my friends. Then my coworkers at my first job became my friends. Then the parents of our kids' friends entered the picture. Along the way, some friendships remain and others drift away. I always feel that people come in and out of your life for a reason, even if only for a short time. When they are in your life, enjoy them and focus on being a good friend in return.

Just as important as making new connections is

knowing when to get rid of someone in your network. Emotionally draining "friends" are not something you need in your life. It is difficult to move away from a relationship that is negative, but do it. This also applies to your children's friends. I have actually told a white lie or two when I did not want my children to interact with a friend who I thought was trouble.

"Sorry, Joe is busy this weekend."

"No, Jack can't have a sleepover."

"Sorry, the boys are busy with sports."

Friends are an important part of your network. They allow you to let your hair down, to laugh, and to share your experiences. Many times I feel I am the only one who is dealing with something. When you open up to others, you realize you are not alone, and that is very comforting. Friends can help you, and you can help them. I am always open to meeting new people and find it fascinating to engage in a new conversation. It is exhilarating to hear something you did not know anything about a few minutes earlier.

Seek out others, and when you are asked to join a small group, give it a try!

BUILD CIRCLES—
PROFESSIONAL
RELATIONSHIPS

My first few jobs after college were with very small start-up companies in Denver. The small companies were fun, but they seemed always to be on the edge of bankruptcy. In fact, two of the companies I worked for went out of business while I was there. In one case, they could not pay me, and in order to settle with me they started giving me items from the office. I felt ridiculous leaving work carrying a microwave with a plant perched on top. The leaves kept falling into my face, and I had to keep blowing at them as I made my way to the car. My boss really appreciated my hard work, and he even offered me his week at a timeshare in the mountains to entice me to stay on until the company could reinvent itself. But I needed a paycheck.

It was 1986. Every time I opened the newspaper to the want ads, the telecommunications companies were the ones advertising lucrative job openings. I took one with a small company that sold telephone equipment, knowing that the company was also financially strapped. Although I was hitting all my sales targets and receiving good commission checks, I knew it wasn't going to last long. The federal government had broken up AT&T in 1984, and as a result, all its operations had been reorganized under seven "Baby Bell" Regional Bell Operating Companies (RBOCs). One of my customers was US West, a recently formed RBOC that was going through massive changes. This meant that it was open to introducing new products and to hiring people from outside the original Bell system. This was my opportunity. I wanted a job that wouldn't pay me in houseplants.

I just needed to get a foot in the door. I was already selling a product to US West but not at the level of management that would be making hiring decisions.

I did not want to get lost in their HR department, so I viewed any chance I had to meet someone who was already employed at US West as an opportunity for me to distribute my résumé. I would give it to anyone who would accept it. I would try to attend events I thought someone from US West would be attending. This was the simplest form of networking. Eventually it worked: Someone was interested in me, and I was called for an interview. It took six months and multiple interviews before I was offered a job. I said yes immediately. Patience is a virtue.

Lunch with Non-Coworkers

Perhaps it's obvious to you by now that I get energy from meeting new people. It invigorates me. I thoroughly enjoy getting out of my bubble to forge new relationships with smart, creative individuals.

Outside influences are critical, and they became even more important as my career advanced. The higher my position at Qwest, the more I leaned outside the company for commiseration and perspective. It is lonely at the top.

Throughout my career, I made it a point to get outside my usual circles at least once a week by going to lunch with someone I didn't work with. Why? Because I knew that by doing this, there would be a great potential to share new ideas, to establish a new connection, or to give someone a referral. My mind-set is this: *Everything leads to something.* Someone can share a concept with you that can lead you to solve something in a way you had not thought of.

> My mind-set is this: *Everything leads to something.*

Misuse of Networking—
Business Card Exchanges

I have no illusions. My tenure in the corporate world has given me many opportunities to see the best and the worst in networking.

At a recent event, for example, a young man sidled up

to me and interrupted a conversation I was having with three attendees with his tart, "Ah, excuse me. Do you have a business card?"

"Yes," I said.

He glanced at my hand, still holding my glass and napkin, then back up to my face. "Ah, may I have one?"

I could feel the stares of the others.

"Well, let's see if we have a reason to exchange cards," I said. "Tell me about yourself."

The young man's eyes widened and he shifted his weight. He wasn't prepared for my resistance. His reaction moved the situation from uncomfortable to something truly awkward. Surprised at my response, he began mumbling something about what he did for a living. Within thirty short seconds it was obvious that no, we had nothing in common, and there was no reason to exchange cards.

I gently interrupted him. "Thank you. It was very nice to meet you, but I don't think I will give you one of my cards." I turned back to the group and picked up our conversation as if it had never been cut off.

Neediness is a turnoff. Approach the process of connecting with others at an event with the idea that you're there to have a good time, and seek to give more than you receive. Don't get in the zone of thinking that you *must* establish a connection at all costs. If no genuine connections are established, see it as part of the process. Smile and be grateful for the opportunity to have met someone new.

A basic understanding of relationship building underlies successful networking.

One of the skills I employ is genuine curiosity to gain an understanding of what the mutual value of the connection could be. I don't try to make connections for the sake of making connections. It makes as much sense as collecting business cards to use as wallpaper or handing them out as if they were flyers.

For instance, if I am meeting someone new in her office, I still want to make that same genuine connection, so I always study the room. I pay attention to my surroundings. A quick scan of the walls or the desk may reveal a common thread, something I know will create an immediate bridge to connect us.

It's all about someone's backstory or personal life that creates an authentic and valuable rapport. The moments when you really connect with someone are the moments to build on and are the moments that may lead to collaborative exchanges later.

Recently we hosted my niece, Megan, who is attending a nearby university. She brought along some of her college sorority sisters, and our small birthday party in her honor was suddenly something of an event. Our house was overrun with young women talking and laughing. Despite the short notice, I served food and chatted with the young women as they came and went. One young woman paused in the chaos to talk with me. My interest was piqued when she told me her major was business. I was hooked. Out of all the young women, she was different: She carried herself confidently and was articulate about her future plans. She was savvy and had a real grasp on what her career might eventually look like. I wiped my hands clean on a towel and jogged out of the kitchen to fetch one of my cards.

Later, as our guests were getting ready to leave, I heard Pete tell her: "I'd hold onto that if I were you. She doesn't give out many of those."

I do hoard my business cards, but not out of judgment or selfishness. I don't refuse to give my business card out because of vanity, either. When I give out my card, it is an invitation to talk or meet in the future. Printed on my cards is my real contact information, and I personally check my own voice mail and email. I know some people who give out their cards to everyone they meet, but for me, sincere and focused connections create less clutter to sort through, maximizing their value. I don't want to waste my time or someone else's.

This is an important principle that the naïve young man had missed in his zeal to get connected.

Follow Up Once You Connect

Another point of networking is this: If you connect with someone, follow up. Make sure to drop an email or make a personal phone call to thank the person who took the time to speak with you or to share his or her story. It's not about constant or frequent contact: By making the effort to strategically reengage with an occasional email or holiday card, for example, you keep the lines of communication and the potential for the future open. Even just a light and congenial message sent via a colleague—"So-and-so says hi!"—shows that you understand the basics of networking etiquette.

I was blown away when I received a thank-you card a week later from the young woman who had visited our home. I smiled from ear to ear and noticed that she had taken the time not only to include a handwritten note, but also to choose the card with care. Wow! She is nineteen and already gets how it works.

It's about give and take. No one gets anywhere on a one-way, dead-end street.

And don't treat networking like a street that goes in only one direction—that is, *your* way, to serve *your* needs.

I remember Christine, my assistant, calling into my

office one afternoon. "Do you know a Trevor? He said he worked for you a few years ago."

Trevor. Trevor. I remembered a Trevor, but my mind was slow in pulling up a face. "Go ahead and put him through," I called back.

Don't treat networking like a street that goes in only one direction—that is, *your* way, to serve *your* needs.

After I picked up the receiver and heard Trevor's voice, I let my forehead fall into my hand. Oh, *that* Trevor! Now I remembered who he was, and in his case, that wasn't a good thing. The pause in recall had suddenly gotten me on a phone call that I never would have taken otherwise. I had worked with Trevor eight years earlier, and it was a relief for my team when he quit to work in a different telecom sales position outside the company. And now he was on the other end of the line, chatting away as if we were friends eager to catch up.

"Trevor, what is it that I can help you with?" I asked when he stopped to take a breath.

"Well, I was calling to set up a meeting with you. You see, my company has this product . . ."

I stopped listening. He had been shallow and unpleasant eight years earlier, and obviously not a lot had changed for him since. Everything that came out of his mouth confirmed what he had been thinking as he'd picked up the phone to dial minutes earlier. He wasn't thinking about me and my company and whether or not his product would fulfill a need—which it didn't. It was about leveraging some weak connection with me in order to make a big score.

"No," I said.

"What?"

"I said no. I am not available for a meeting. But thank you for the phone call. I wish you well." I hung up the phone without saying good-bye.

This is not how networking works. Networking is not appearing in someone's office and shouting,

Ta-da! Networking is not pitching a product or asking for help. You cannot capitalize on a relationship that never existed. You do not attempt to use people for your own personal gain. Think about it. How long does a normal friendship last when a friend only calls you up for favors or special considerations? It is very, very bad manners to reach out to someone solely when you want something from him or her.

Networking is not about making people into human vending machines. Networking is about sourcing.

Networking

If staying in the loop means being at the opening of a museum, a restaurant, or even an envelope, I'm in. For me, the initial hurdle to networking is as basic as walking in the doors of the event.

But whether you're a seasoned networker like me or new to the networking scene, here are four additional tips to keep in mind that will serve you well.

- Remove distractions and any discomforts. Appearance is important. How you present yourself is reflective of your ideas. Dress as if you take yourself as seriously as you would like your audience to. And wear a comfortable pair of shoes.

- View networking as a type of soft sales pitch, where you're not hard selling yourself. Networking makes it possible to meet people and develop relationships based on a mutual interest that can lead to open doors in the future.

- The entrance: Take a friend, even an acquaintance. You can meet ahead of time and walk into a room together. Work your way into a room: Start at the door and head right or left; look for someone to connect with or get a drink. There is an art to finding the initial person.

- If you spend the time to connect with someone, even fifteen minutes, and you don't follow up with it, it is a waste. Make the connection last longer by creating another reason to communicate. You need a way to continue the conversation.

Our abilities to identify resources in our everyday interactions can enable us to accomplish more, find opportunities, and provide needed safety nets and support as well. Finding those connections that enrich us can be done in almost all social situations. This feeds into the greater idea that, collectively, we function better with assistance from others. Our connections are our source for creativity, new ideas, help, and success.

Build circles around you, both in your personal and in your professional worlds.

NAVIGATING POLITICAL SITUATIONS AT THE OFFICE

The circles you have created are your strongest ally when dealing with the political landscape at the office. You cannot avoid the politics: It is just a part of work.

The system is set up to foster competitiveness, and this is good when everyone has the same goals or ethics. But I guarantee there will always be *someone* who will play nastier than the rest. Not everyone will be out to get you, but there will always be one.

You'll know this person because he or she is the one who will always try to steal your work, who will be jealous, or who would do anything to be able to replace you on the project you're on—not to mention wanting to take credit for whatever you've accomplished. At times, in the workplace, it can feel like survival of the fittest. I learned this sad fact early in my career. My idealistic outlook fizzled in a brilliant flash of realization when I received my first knife in the back, and I learned that not everyone was going to play by the rules. I needed to set up a good offensive without compromising my ethics for those days when I felt like I was in an open field, dodging multiple daggers.

There's Always One in the Room

Chances are that if you get more than four people together in a room, one of them probably has a hidden agenda. Not a pretty concept. Accepting the idea that "there's always one" will give you a better chance of navigating the natural competitiveness of the corporate world.

In my world, in order to dodge and weave in a manner that kept any major blows from landing, you needed to be involved with something new: a new market, a new project, a new division, something—anything—out of the ordinary. The funding for these projects was always better, and the work was exciting and cutting edge. This was the most likely way you'd be able to come out on top, and that kind of peace of mind was worth fighting for.

It was in these areas that you scored points for being involved with something high profile. High profile meant projects that would lead to your being interviewed or written up by the press, to having the board of directors ask about you, or to your wielding the ability to hire consultants and to invest in advancing technology. I worked long hours, used the skills I had gathered early on, refused to compromise my ethics, and went for each new challenge. Later, there were opportunities to speak at public venues, offer opinions, and become an expert quoted in trade publications.

Similarly, high-profile projects made you a bit more impervious to the slings and arrows thrown at you. But in order to be asked in on any groundbreaking effort, you had to first fight to be higher up in the pecking order so that you would be the one the decision makers would ask. That's where the groundwork that I had laid—networking around the office, making myself available and known—paid off. I arranged dinners and lunches or went out for drinks with the people I admired and could learn from. I tried to figure out who the other people were who would also be interested in these new projects. This took an investment of time (and I made sure this was the right use of that time), but it was worth the effort.

But it's dangerous to assume that as you reach the higher levels of the business world, the pettiness dissipates. Even at the top, there is and will always be that One. (Insert scream of frustration here.) At this level, the One has usually spent years perfecting techniques to become a mastermind of sabotage.

In one particular case, the One was an archenemy who declared out-and-out war on me. My nemesis and I had a form of pretense in the way we treated each other, but that quickly wore off as he went beyond anything I had experienced before. His approach to his self-declared position of "advisor to the CEO" was to poke at and point out everyone else's weaknesses, which meant that he was constantly digging for information to use as ammunition for his reports and assessments. He didn't shy away from twisting facts and inventing alternate results and false matrixes about the efficiency of my departments, and then he would report to my boss that my division really wasn't running as well as I had claimed.

I would go to my regular meeting with my boss, and he would ask me: "How is that *such and such* going?" *Wait a minute!* I would freeze up because *such and such* wasn't part of the agenda.

"Fine," I would answer. *I wasn't supposed to have a report about that for another week.* "We have a couple of issues we need to get after, but it'll all work out." *Especially by next week, when I was supposed to report about it.*

"Well, keep me updated about it," he would say with a sniff.

"Of course."

After awhile, I figured out that he was being fed erroneous information, and I figured out who was feeding it to him. So the next time he asked about anything off our current agenda or tried to casually go off topic during a meeting, I would blurt out, "So what did *he* tell you?"

This got me into a bit of hot water with my boss. My sensitivity was justified, but all he heard was me being defensive, and more than once he accused me of trying to cover or protect my own group rather than dealing with the glaring issues I was so obviously ignoring. In a way, he was right. I *was* trying to ignore the whole thing, because no one likes to deal with false accusations!

I was constantly blindsided, and I struggled to get out ahead of my foe instead of having to defend and point out everything he reported that was false. I tried not to feel victimized as he smiled and lied to me in the beginning. When it got really bad, I tried to confront him, to rationalize with him about what he was doing. I already knew this wouldn't work because of my earlier blunders at confrontation in my career, but like everyone else, I'd get drawn in once in a while. I cornered him once in the hall and boldly told him that what he was doing was wrong. When I did, I knew he had won some sort of victory over me, and he knew it, too. He smirked, bobbed his head at me, and said he was doing nothing wrong. That the only reason I was being defensive was that he was actually right! If I felt I was misunderstanding the situation, it was because there was simply a different way to look at it. *Huh!* What a waste of time!

I was on my heels for a good year during the time my boss believed him and not me.

I needed to get ahead of the issue. I knew the only way to protect myself and my employees was to take away his power. I stopped being upset by what he reported, and instead I began to pay attention to what my boss seemed to care about most in those reports. I dissected that information until a pattern of his interests began to emerge. Once I saw it, I began to get data to my boss ahead of schedule so there was already other information to draw from when the One sauntered into his office. The goal was to counter him, like having an antidote ready before the poison could set in.

That is where my many years of relationship building helped me. Many others could see what was happening and wanted to help me get out of the situation. Suddenly, information was flowing to me earlier than the due date, or side conversations were giving me a "heads up" on potential issues. I also needed to cut off the One's flow of information and plug the leaks. Previously, my team members had been caught off guard when he had circumvented my authority and asked them for numbers. They had supplied him with whatever data he had requested. During a quick strategy session with my group, we found our solution. It was simple: My team agreed to tell him they were sorry, but they had too much on their plates. "You're going to have to call Teresa and ask her about that," they told him. He never called.

Unfortunately, I was not the only person he zeroed in on. He went after other divisions as well. We all became wary of what he would send down the pike next, and with his busy slash-and-dash life, he soon alienated any other allies he might have won.

I knew it would only be a matter of time before the system would resolve the situation. You just have to out-last the crazy. A good system will allow those who spew negativity to last a certain length of time before they are the ones spewed out. In this case, my boss apologized for misjudging the situation and for mistreating me after he came to see what was really going on.

> A good system will allow those who spew negativity to last a certain length of time before they are the ones spewed out. You just have to outlast the crazy.

"I'm sorry I didn't support you and that I dragged you through the wringer," he finally said. I accepted his apology, though I wish it had been different. And it *could* have been different.

During this tough time, I was surprised at the individuals who emerged to assist me. People that I didn't think I was close to stopped by to ask, "What can I do to help?" I took that lesson and helped them when the tables were turned, or gave them advice based on my experience. Again, the circles I had built were now my strength.

Read the Tea Leaves

Tassology. The art of reading tea leaves.

At the bottom of a great cup of tea, the leaves that give the brew its flavor are left behind. Legend has it that the study of such tea leaves will show you insights into your future and will help you map out a course of action.

I believe our actions every day leave behind the same kind of remnant as is found in the bottom of a cup of tea, and that if we study those actions, it can help us navigate essential parts of our life.

My friend Robin and I talk all the time about the need to read the tea leaves our respective work leaves us with. We both agree that an essential corporate survival skill is learning to study any individual's behavior—be it your boss, your customer, your peer, or your own staff.

First, I learned to watch. I had a particularly indecisive boss at one point. My observations led me to develop a working theory of what made him tick and how he got ticked off. The conversation in my head went something like this: "Well, he made X decision quickly last week but not today. Why the difference?"

I would apply whatever remedy I thought would cure his indecisiveness, and I would hope for the best. If I failed, I stepped back and observed some more. It was all about trial and error. Think strategy. There is almost always an alternative to try. If my first approach didn't work, I'd try another. When things didn't go my way, I'd be frustrated, but I'd still choose to observe more and reflect.

Failure would come only if I accepted defeat.

I finally figured out that no matter how many times my theories were wrong, the one truth I could bank on was that my boss was not going to change. Pushing for change with a boss who is already super-stressed-out passes the tension down the chain of command, and this creates a toxic environment. It's a cascade effect.

When I needed my boss to make a decision, I carefully laid my case out to him in a way that would propel him into action.

I called it managing up.

But a funny thing happened: He eventually learned that he was *being managed*. He was resentful at first because he was under the impression that I was trying to manipulate him. I wasn't! As time progressed and he noticed how painless and seamless our interactions had become, his glares wore off, and I noticed that he was more relaxed with me than with other executives. He began to expect that type of style from me, and he appreciated that I was trying to make his life easier.

It grew on him, and he found it easier to reach his decisions.

On the other hand, I had another boss who never got over my approach and who detested and loathed it. He hated being *managed*, he said, but I didn't have a choice.

I learned to maneuver around even that roadblock, however. If he was moody, I did us both a favor by shortening the list and only addressing what was critical at that moment, for that day. If I had an agenda for our meeting and I could tell the stars were not aligned for a successful outcome, I'd cut things off my list and reschedule them until later. The papers I brought for him to sign would magically disappear under a book or my seat.

At some point, he became suspicious. "Didn't you

come in with a stack of papers for me to sign? Brenda said you had some forms for me."

I faked confusion. "No, not today."

"Let me see that sheet of paper you're holding." He reached over the desk.

"This?" I folded the piece of paper in half and shoved it into my folder. "That's just my grocery list for the ride home."

I think I heard him growl.

I also got in good with my bosses' administrative assistants. The people in that role always knew what was and wasn't a good idea depending on the day. I used them to get advance intelligence, if possible. They were tea leaf readers as well, after all.

Any time I failed, it was because I chose to ignore the tea leaves—or perhaps I hadn't drunk enough tea!

Working with Men and Women

I celebrate the accomplishments of women. I see the value in both men and women's achievements. But I've been accused of being exclusionary of men. I just laugh.

In a field dominated with men who unapologetically congratulate one another's accomplishments with slaps on the back while toddling around a golf course, bonding over bogies and handicaps, I chose to create an alternative venue to provide the same recognition for what the women at my office had accomplished.

I chose to use my home as a haven where we could highlight the incredible accomplishments of my gender. Instead of golf clubs, we bonded over hors d'oeuvres, drinks, and common experiences. Regardless of their department or whether I worked with them personally, I wanted women to be celebrated.

Most importantly, it wasn't about my gathering women around me; it was about these women gathering around each other and having the opportunity to recognize and to know one another. I wanted them to learn they could depend on and be encouraged by the show of support.

I did not exclude men from these events because I had an ax to grind with them. Point of fact: I don't hate men and I don't participate in man bashing. EVER. I've exited rooms and left luncheons early because of it. Too often, generalized oppression by men can be used as an excuse for women to verbally excoriate or ridicule specific men. Men are sometimes cast as the scapegoat for all that goes wrong for a woman.

What I do know is that by bringing women together to celebrate in a space where the spirit of women can thrive, we can emphasize our strengths, and we can better promote our accomplishments and inspire new ones.

I've always had the sense that one woman, alone, represents all women in her performance on the job.

In these celebratory gatherings, it was refreshing not only to talk about our successes but also to hear us debating issues among ourselves. Women should be the driving force behind these conversations—that is, mentors and mentees discussing the merits and drawbacks of each issue. Women can be their own worst enemy in the workplace and in life, but they can also be a force of positive change.

I believed in being available to women to help, coach, support, advise, and so on. Even if I was criticized for mentoring and accused of favoring women over men, it wasn't for the laughable reason of preferring my gender. It was out of a desire to keep another young woman from becoming a cliché. So I leaned into women more than I did men. I felt like I needed it, and so did they.

> Even if I was criticized for mentoring and accused of favoring women over men, it wasn't for the laughable reason of preferring my gender. It was out of a desire to keep another young woman from becoming a cliché.

Ed Mueller, CEO during the end of my tenure at Qwest, had an accurate grasp on how I managed to balance being what he called "one of the girls" in a man's world. Ed told me once that he saw me as temperamentally middle of the road, not trying to be like a man while still not being a stereotypical woman. He saw me as decisive and thoughtful. He said I was reasonable and that I understood male behavior. He told me he liked that I was never an excuse maker and that once he had highlighted a problem, he didn't have to worry about that problem again. And most important, I didn't hold grudges. The last item he pinned on women in general, along with the ability to be too catty and to take things too personally. He said I also diverged from my female counterparts in that I was responsive to criticism, even as I demanded that my opinion be heard. But once my opinion was voiced, I went forward with the decision without a chip on my shoulder, even if I was overruled. I could move forward.

I appreciated the nuances he picked up on in how I conducted myself at work. This is what I wanted to pass on to the women I mentored. I did take things personally, but I didn't show it. I went home having the same number of bad days as others, but maintaining my professional equilibrium was important to me and always paid dividends.

EPILOGUE

My departure from Qwest felt like it arrived in the same harried way that had sent me rushing off to the elementary school years earlier, not wanting to miss lunch with my son. I was marking the end of a fast-paced era in my life. Standing in the doorway of my office, I turned off the lights of my now-barren executive office. Earlier, boxes—my plaques, awards, and accolades all neatly tucked inside—had removed my personality from its walls. I had had many offices over my twenty-three-year tenure, but having just led a telecom giant through an acquisition, facilitating the $22 billion process, and navigating the complexities of a large corporate merger, this was to be my last. I headed down the hallway of the fifty-second floor to the bank of elevators. While I cherished all the varied experiences of my job, it was my home life that had grafted the energy and soul into what could have been an empty corporate existence.

I entered the elevator and pushed the lobby button. My time was up, and I had somewhere else to be.

After I left Qwest, I decided to turn down offers outside of Denver, against conventional wisdom, for the most important reason. I knew that if my sons or my husband were miserable, even if I was thrilled, I could not be an effective leader, nor would I feel whole. I couldn't be anything other than what I was, and that truth had been in evidence throughout my entire tenure at Qwest. At the end of the day, I am successful because of, not in spite of, the ones I have at home.

And I wasn't about to fix what wasn't broken.

It is not pretty or perfect. No magical formula or secret checklist makes working while being a wife and mother devoid of hardship. But it can be done and it can be done well, without feeling split in two. As women, if we do not redefine this harshness that we are projecting on ourselves, we are not going to have to worry just about some perceived failing grade. Ultimately, it will be about why, collectively, we give up. We can't be all things to all people, but above all, we can't divide ourselves in two.

Throw out the idea of perfection and the belief that a magic checklist for someone's career actually exists. There are no secrets. It is simply about working hard. Working hard is the mainstay to a successful career, and it's the same for home. It is about one life, one calendar— not bifurcating yourself. You need to be all in.

Be who you are all the time and work harder than everyone else to make it work, even if that includes your spouse. There will be times when you are giving more than your share of a supposedly 50/50 arrangement. And it is guaranteed that there will be times when your part- ner is giving more than you, too. Just be committed and make it work.

Endurance is the key.

Take the time to celebrate, even if you're just cele- brating that you made it to Wednesday. Don't you enjoy going to a great party? Why not create your own parties? Celebrate yourself and the things you did accomplish instead of focusing on what did not happen. I have gotten into the habit of sending flowers often. I send them to many women, sometimes for a small reason and sometimes just to say thanks for listening. Go ahead and send them to yourself once in a while!

You can feel good about both home and work. The answers are within you.

A SPECIAL MESSAGE TO MY SONS

Dear Jack and Joe,

When I started the journey of writing this book, my intent was to give hope and encouragement to young women. I wanted to help them believe that they can have both a successful career and an extraordinary personal life. My hope is that working women will find peace rather than searching for "balance." Life is not an equation that can be balanced; it's a series of interactions, lessons learned, and just plain living!

I know when you read early versions of this book and now that you've read this final publication, you have had many emotions: surprise, laughter, shock, sadness, amusement, to name a few. I truly appreciate how the two of you, along with your father, accommodated and supported my drive to write this book.

As you grew with me in my professional career, you witnessed my early mornings, late nights, and traveling. Remember how many times I took you to my office? How many times I dressed you up and showed you off at work parties or events? (Joe was the only one who actually enjoyed wearing a suit and tie at age five!)

Of course, you also enjoyed the upside: front-row tickets for sporting events and concerts, and flights in the corporate jet. How many moms have a helicopter pick them up at their house so they can tour the state of Colorado? Remember the time I threw out the first pitch at the Rockies baseball game? You practiced with me for hours at home and then I totally fumbled when it came time to execute. You rolled with it all and never questioned it.

I have a few wishes for you as you continue to grow:

I wish that you'll each find a career that makes you happy, and that you enjoy the work you do every day.

I wish that if you decide to marry, you will support whatever career your wife chooses—whether it involves staying at home or working outside of the home—as you have observed with me and your father.

I wish that some of the stories I've shared in this book will help you as you begin your working life.

I wish that you will find a person to love as much as I love your father.

I wish that if you decide to become fathers, you will be blessed with healthy, loving children, as I have been blessed with the two of you.

Our journey together has just begun, and I can't wait to see how the two of you continue to grow as young men. You will be wonderful at whatever you do.

All of my love,
Mom

ABOUT THE AUTHOR

TERESA TAYLOR is a nationally recognized telecom executive who brings integrity, focus, vision, and agility to corporate leadership. She has earned her reputation for building and managing cohesive teams, inspiring loyalty, managing through conflict, and embracing change.

Taylor advises companies, government agencies, and other enterprises on vision, strategy, operations, and public affairs. She serves on the board of directors for First Interstate BancSystem, Inc., a financial services holding company with $7.3 billion in assets headquartered in Billings, Montana, as well as the board of directors for NiSource, Inc., a Fortune 500 natural gas and electricity storage and transmission company based in Merrillville, Indiana.

Additionally, Taylor is an executive adviser to Governor John Hickenlooper and serves on the Colorado Economic Development Commission. She also serves on the Global Leadership Council for Colorado State University's College of Business and is a member of the Board of Directors for the Colorado Technology Association.

In 2009, Taylor was named the chief operating officer of Qwest, a $12 billion national media and telecommunications company headquartered in Denver, Colorado. She directed the strategy and daily operations of thirty thousand people in field support, technical development, sales, marketing, customer support, and IT systems in India and the United States. Taylor was responsible for the strategic planning and execution of serving consumer, wholesale, small business, and large business customers, including the federal government. She represented the company in public and community venues, as well as with Wall Street and investors. During her tenure, she achieved 58 percent growth in stock performance

About the Author

and outperformed all peers. In 2011, she led the telecom giant through an acquisition, facilitating the $22 billion process and navigating the complexities of a large corporate merger.

Previously, Ms. Taylor held numerous executive positions at Qwest, including executive vice president of business markets, chief administrative officer, executive vice president of wholesale, and executive vice president of products. Prior to her twenty-three years with Qwest, she worked with several start-up technology companies.

Taylor has been featured in a number of national business publications, including the *New York Times* and the *Wall Street Journal*. She is sought after as a speaker on topics including leadership, economic development, and innovation.

She resides in Golden, Colorado, with her husband and two sons.

INDEX

INDEX

greed vs. integrity, 138–42

Index

INDEX